Advocacy, Self-Advocacy and Special Needs

Edited by Philip Garner and Sarah Sandow

David Fulton Publishers

Lond

D0299999

David Fulton Publishers Ltd
2 Barbon Close, London WC1N 3JX

First published in Great Britain by
David Fulton Publishers 1995

British Library Cataloguing in Publication Data

A catalogue record for this book is available from the British Library

ISBN 1–85346–349–3

Camera Ready Copy by Philip Garner and Sarah Sandow
Printed in Great Britain by BPC Books and Journals, Exeter

CONTENTS

The Contributors.

Robert Catt is a Senior Lecturer in Education at Brunel University.

David Coulby is Professor of Education at Bath College of Higher Education.

Jacquie Coulby is Headteacher of Batheaston Church of England Primary School, Bath.

Philip Garner is a Senior Lecturer in Special Education at Brunel University.

Barbara Gersch is Senior Education Officer with the London Borough of Waltham Forest.

Irvine Gersch is an Educational Psychologist with the London Borough of Waltham Forest.

Rena Harris-Cooksley is Head of Learning Support at Bentley Wood High School, London Borough of Harrow.

Sarah Sandow is Reader in Education at Brunel University

Tom Sweeney is a Senior Lecturer in Education at Brunel University

Acknowledgements

We have relied on the continued support of many colleagues and friends during the time we have been producing this book. We would like to thank them all. Their encouragement at strategic times was essential.

INTRODUCTION

Advocacy is the representation of the views, feelings and interests of one person or group of people by another individual or organisation. During the last twenty years there has been a steady increase in the number of individuals and groups who have sought to improve the educational opportunities of children who have special educational needs (SEN). Some advocacy in SEN, as in the case of many large national charities, is underpinned by a belief in social justice and equality of opportunity. Many individuals, on the other hand, are involved because of direct personal or familial experience of learning difficulties, such as parents.

Self-advocacy is the action or utterance of a person on their own behalf without the intervention of another. The shift in focus from advocacy to self-advocacy is a natural extension of the process of empowerment, and mirrors the experience of other groups in society who have sought to replace the intervention of concerned others with their own direct action.

Preparing to write this book, we first identified a list of words which seemed to be commonly associated with advocacy and self-advocacy in the general context of SEN. We then asked a group of 36 teachers concerned with SEN to brainstorm words and ideas associated with the words we selected. Table 1 shows some of their responses.

What is apparent in this exercise is that many of the terms relating to the involvement of those who have learning difficulty in decision making are seen as having broad application. In this book we are not seeking to make finite definitions of advocacy or self-advocacy, nor to promote one at the expense of the other. It is our belief that terminology is of less importance than principle.

The significance of advocacy lies in the recognition that a person's own skills may not include the ability to speak for him or herself, for intellectual, social, emotional, developmental or physical reasons. The recognition of an individual's right to a hearing despite any or all of these difficulties places advocacy within the context of human rights. The significance of self-

SEN AND RIGHTS	SEN AND ADVOCACY	SEN AND SELF-ADVOCACY	SEN AND EMPOWERMENT
Right of access (Warnock)	Parents:	Control of one's own life/learning/education	Pupil choice, power to children
Integration	Fight	Independence	Autonomy
Equality of opportunity	Appeal	Self-discipline	Independence
Enabling, facilitate	Stamina	Self-assessment/evaluation	Knowledge
Parental rights, Involvement	Understand system	Self-reliance	Freedom
Responsibility	Access	Self-esteem	Self-worth
Rights of child	Self belief	Confidence	Self-esteem
Expectatons	Clear aim	Direction	Being in control of their learning
		Motivation	Ownership
	Teaching staff/ other staff:	Planning for own needs	Negotiation
	Caution	Emotional independence	Equal opportunity
		Awareness of freedom of choice	Differentiation

SEN AND EQUALITY OF OPPORTUNITY	SEN AND EQUITY	SEN AND PUPIL PARTICIPATION	
Access	Differentiatiion,	No motivation, no participation	
Equity	Equity *not* equality,	Interest	
Acceptance	'Special' not 'equal'	Confidence safety and security	
Differentiation	Impossible	Pupil taking responsibility	
Equal treatment, *same*	Attempts at equity create imbalance	Empowerment	
Experiences		Want to	
Alternative activities		Need to	
Differentiated			
Special provision			

Table 1 : Summary of teachers' brainstorm on advocacy, self-advocacy and related terms advocacy lies in its power to increase the sum of human happiness through extending the power of personal representation to all individuals. It reduces their vulnerability to exploitation and maximises their self-esteem in an increasingly complex and sometimes hostile society.

While advocacy will always be useful and often necessary, self-advocacy is essential if individuals are to have genuine power over their own lives. However, self-advocacy needs to be based in self-understanding and empathy, otherwise empowerment can become tyranny. In situations where self-advocacy and even advocacy are disallowed, some individuals may substitute anti-social, aggressive or destructive behaviours, or seek inappropriate gratification, and others may exist in a condition of learned helplessness which is inimical to their own or others' fulfilment.

A feature of the history of psychology, sociology and education during the past one hundred and fifty years has been the gradual acceptance of an increasing range of individual differences, and the concomitant expansion of human rights. The gradual extension of the franchise, the foundation of universal elementary, and, later secondary education, the emancipation of women and the formal elimination of racial discrimination have brought with them a steadily increasing recognition of first the needs, and then the rights, of almost the whole population. There remain some groups, however, which are still left largely without influence. The largest of these groups is children, and a subset of this group is children with SEN. Ironically, this group appears to be increasing in number, a side-effect of the increasingly inclusive educational policies of the past 25 years or so. Before 1971, some 0.5% of the school population were excluded from 'normal' education. A further 1.5% passed their school lives in special schools, and ordinary schools were assumed to cater successfully for the rest of the population.

After the 1981 Act and its precursor the Warnock Report (DES, 1978) there was a growing recognition that far more children, up to 20%, would have more or less serious difficulties at some time during their school life However, not only was it now understood that they had needs, it was also suggested that they had incapacities which prevented or interfered with their contribution to, and participation in, child and adult life.

Our society is ambivalent about children. We have treated them as incompetent and irresponsible, but at the same time elevated children as vital and demanding consumers, albeit through their parents, of all the goods and services which maintain the economy of the country. Food, drink, clothing, toys, television, computers, are all dependant on the child consumer. It is not surprising that children find it difficult to sustain positive relations with each other and with the adults who attempt to control them. Children who are identified as having SEN must find it even more difficult to relate to others in a way described by Rogers (1969) as 'accurate empathy' and 'unconditional positive regard'. So advocacy, and more significantly self-advocacy, is at least as important for this group as it is for all other young people.

This book is divided into three parts. Issues of context and principle are dealt with by the two editors in *Section One*. Here we discuss the dilemmas and the potential for advocacy and self-advocacy. In *Section Two* are included contributions from teachers and other professionals which describe a number of practical approaches designed to empower children and young people in school and beyond. In *Section Three* we attempt to gather together both theoretical and practical aspects of advocacy and self-advocacy in two chapters which focus upon continuing professional and institutional development.

We need to understand how advocacy and self-advocacy can be developed in the future, and how attention to these issues can encourage both individual teachers and the 'inclusive school' to flourish. We have designed this book as both a reflective and practical resource for teachers, but one which hopefully does not minimise the issues or ignore the difficulties involved in such developments. Empowerment is an alarming, dangerous and thrilling enterprise. It is what education is for.

Chapter 1.1

THE CONTEXT FOR ADVOCACY AND SELF-ADVOCACY

Advocacy and particularly self-advocacy are currently fashionable. But why now? What is it about the 1990s which leads us to discuss self-advocacy in such detail? And why specifically for those with SEN?

It appears that there have been socio-political, legal and educational reasons for this development. The history of educational initiatives will be dealt with in Chapter 1.3. This chapter will look at the interplay between political and legal developments, and the social and educational implications.

Politics

First, a system of government has been established in western capitalist economies, particularly in Britain and the United States, which regards State intervention as potentially suspect, probably expensive and almost always counter-productive. The 'nanny state' is perceived as inimical to growth, strength and independence. In Britain, systems which in the past protected the most vulnerable from exploitation, such as the Wages Councils, have been abandoned, bar one. Provisions of the Social Chapter of the Maastricht Treaty regarded as fairly uncontroversial by other European Union members, including measures such as worker representation in industry and reasonable working hours, were rejected by the UK government as striking at the foundations of the entrepreneurial society. In 1994, the Secretary of State for Employment, Michael Portillo, abolished the system which favoured the awarding of government contracts to employers with large numbers of disabled workers. This has followed a determined campaign by government to resist disability rights legislation despite powerful support for it inside and beyond Parliament. All of these measures are examples of the current enthusiasm for the rights of the individual (especially the powerful individual) at the expense of the community.

In a passionate article, Wolfensberger (1994) identifies a number of issues which he regards as indicators of 'modernist' thinking. Modernism, he writes,

> exalts individualism to the point of idolatry of the self...(it) exalts selfishness and selfcentredness rather than seeing these as a vice. ...this results quite logically in a value relativism and a utilitarian ethic which values things (including people) on the basis of how much they are of benefit to others, and/or how much they cost.

Those who are not and cannot be 'cost effective', he warns, (see also Warnock, 1991) include the handicapped (sic), the poor, prisoners, derelicts, native and migrant populations, the elderly, the chronic and terminally sick.

Where governments see their role as minimalist, in that they resist intervention to protect the vulnerable from an excess of utilitarianism, and controlling, in the sense of protecting the 'majority' from the expensive dispossessed, the only way in which individual people can influence events is by banding together as pressure groups to promote change in their favour. In other words, they must compete for 'scarce resources' against other, perhaps equally deserving groups. So the political system itself generates advocacy and self-advocacy. This means that some very disparate groups are identified as 'minorities': women, blacks, gays, the disabled, purely because they must fight among themselves for recognition and rights. As they fight, they create a league table of 'deserving causes'.

As a result of the pressure on resources, and also of the identification of individuals as 'customers' in a market economy, groups have developed to press a case for particular sections of the community; for without such pressure, nothing, in a demand-and-supply world can be provided. Lipsky (1980) identified the 'street level bureaucrat', the main point of contact between the customer and the provider, who is subject to enormous pressures simply to cope with the workload imposed on him or her. Hudson (1989) demonstrates how these workers seek to control the clientele by establishing in them a lowered expectation of service. It follows that in such a climate, those who shout loudest will obtain the best services, and those who are best able to shout are the articulate and the moderately wealthy, accustomed to the role of consumer. (The influence of the 'dyslexia lobby' will be examined in Chapter 2.4). To begin with, these groups were advocates, arguing, often within the framework of various charities, for a range of disadvantaged populations. During recent years the advocates have given way to self-advocates. Whereas advocates argue for help, support and equal opportunities, self-advocates argue for rights and equity. Gipps and Murphy (1994) distinguish between equality and equity, and their discussion relates closely to the way self-advocacy has developed. Equal opportunity implies the provision of facilities for a minority such as the disabled, where such facilities have been lacking, and the responsibility of the disabled to take advantage of them. Equity, on the other hand implies the restructuring of what is offered in such a way that the final outcome is equally attainable. In one case, the responsibility is on the individual, in the other it is on the provider. For example, in the early days of educational integration, it was thought enough to include the child with Down's Syndrome in the mainstream classroom, from which he or she had previously been excluded. The responsibility was his or hers to learn. When such children could no longer 'cope' they could be removed to the special school. Later it was realised that more than simple exposure was required if integration were to succeed (Stobart, 1986). Currently the commercialisation of education is promoted as consistent with equal opportunity, (although even that may not be universal) but it cannot be consonant with equity, unless the consumers of education, the disabled, can persuade the provider to alter the product to suit them. So the market orientation of right-wing political regimes itself generates self-advocacy.

Legal issues

We structure our society in layers and each layer has its identified rules, enshrined in unwritten codes and protocols, and ultimately in laws. Local authorities have bye-laws which in turn are sanctioned by national government. That government is constrained to an extent by international (and in our case by European) laws. At each level laws are designed which depend for their effectiveness on testable definitions and functions. There is a constant tension between the construction of definitions which are as inclusive as possible and the constriction of them to be as restrictive as possible. These tensions exist both between the various layers of legislation (as for example between the British and European Parliaments) and within a layer of government, where different ministries, or even successive ministers in the same departments draft laws which are incompatible with one another. In education, we may cite the 1980 Education Act which extended the rights of parents to choose schools, and the 1981 Act which removed that right from the parents of children with special needs once those children had received the 'protection' of a statement

If we read the thirty articles of the United Nations Universal Declaration of Human Rights we see instantly that they are honoured more in the breach than in the observance. Nevertheless they provide a standard against which we may measure national laws. Those which relate to the rights of children include:

> Article 26   (1) Everyone has the right to education. Education shall be free, at least in the elementary and fundamental stages. Elementary education shall be compulsory. Technical and professional education shall be made generally available and higher education shall be equally accessible to all on the basis of merit.

In this country elementary (primary and secondary) education may be compulsory, but more than 3,000 children are permanently excluded from it (NERS, 1992). Of these, 12.5% had statements of special educational needs. In the whole school population about 2.5% have statements. Further, 8% were Afro-Caribbean, whereas this group represents about 2% of the whole school population. So this 'compulsory' education is more likely to be denied to already disadvantaged groups than to others.

The availability of higher education to all regardless of income is also becoming increasingly problematic, with the reduction of student grants to a level which even parents of very modest means are required to supplement, and the introduction of student loans, the repayment of which becomes increasingly difficult in an age of unemployment. Access, in the narrower physical sense, also restricts the availability of higher education for disabled students.

> Article 26(2) Education shall be directed to the full development of the human personality and to the strengthening of respect for human rights and fundamental freedoms. It shall promote understanding, tolerance and friendship among all nations, racial and religious groups, and shall further the activities of the United Nations for the maintenance of peace.

In this context, the disappearance of 'peace studies' as an element in school or university courses, following its denigration in traditional circles, is notable.

Article 26(3) Parents have a prior right to choose the kind of education that shall be given to their children.

As we have seen, this does not apply to those who have children with special educational needs *with statements*, but it also fails to apply to those who, increasingly, since the advent of grant-maintained schools and multiple applications to secondary schools, are unable to secure places for their children in even their third choice of school.

Article 7 All are equal before the law and are entitled without any discrimination to equal protection of the law. All are entitled to equal protection against any discrimination in violation of this declaration and against any incitement to such discrimination.

The inequalities cited above are evidence that such *de facto* discrimination exists.

We should note also:

Article 21 (2) Everyone has the right of equal access to public service in his country.

and

Article 27 (1) Everyone has the right freely to participate in the cultural life of the community, to enjoy the arts and to share in scientific advancement and its benefits.

The assumption here is that non-participation is an active choice of the individual, but where equality of opportunity and failures in provision occur, such as result from the vagaries of the Arts Council, large sections of the population are denied access to 'cultural life'.

We also need to be aware of the United Nations Convention on the Rights of the Child (1989). In particular, we may note:

Article 12 (1) States Parties shall assure to the child who is capable of forming his or her own views the right to express those views freely in all matters affecting the child, the views of the child being given due weight in accordance with the age and maturity of the child.

Article 12 (2) For this purpose the child shall in particular be provided the opportunity to be heard in any judicial or administrative proceedings affecting the child, either directly or through a representative or an appropriate body, in a manner consistent with the procedural rules of national law.

and

Article 13 (1) The child shall have the right to freedom of expression; this right shall include the freedom to seek, receive and impart information and ideas of all kinds, regardless of frontiers, either orally or in print, in the form of art or any other medium of the child's choice.

These statements too are rendered problematic in English law. Rosenbaum and Newell (1991) pointed out that responsibility for matters affecting children are spread across at least seven different government departments. This often leads to contradictions about the rights of children and their parents. Because of the lack of coordination and resulting confusion, Rosenbaum and Newell, in a monograph produced for the Gulbenkian Foundation, proposed the appointment of a 'Children's Rights Commissioner' who would promote the interests of children and young people. Among other functions, such a Commissioner would specifically promote self-advocacy, by giving grants to self-advocacy groups, and by receiving direct input from children and young people.

Earlier, Franklin (1986) even argued for the extension of the franchise to children, suggesting that the age barrier is arbitrary and illogical and that objections based on children's inexperience, gullibility and irresponsibility could be as easily made to the adult franchise (and were, of course, made to justify the withholding of the franchise from women under 30 until 1928).

Legally, children's rights within schools are complicated by the fact that teachers are regarded as 'in loco parentis' (Jeffs, 1986) Therefore any participative action by schoolchildren takes place in a context of paternalism and indulgence. There is a conflict here between the adumbrated rights in the UN convention and the privileges accorded in many schools.

This conflict between two principles is also illustrated by the arrangements under the 1989 Children Act. The Act states that the views of children are to be ascertained and taken into account in any proceedings, and in courts a 'guardian ad litem' and a solicitor appointed to look after their interests, and to present their point of view. It is therefore wholly consonant with the UN convention. However, the view, as transmitted by the guardian, may not be exactly as given by the child. For instance, if a child says at one point, 'I wish to live with my father' and at another, 'I wish to live with my mother', the guardian must identify what is in the child's best interests, and decide which of those statements to take into account. It is rare for a child to address the court directly themselves, but there are ways in which this can be facilitated, described in Chapter 2.5. Thus the intervention of the adult cannot be free from some interpretive bias, and it is always possible that a poor decision will be made. The popular view, that the Children Act entitles children to 'divorce their parents', is wholly erroneous, despite recent well-publicised cases.

However, the 1989 Act does represent the first serious attempt to include the views of children in any decisions about their welfare. It has been, despite the caveat, at its most successful in court proceedings. However, children's rights to a view about their educational experience are a different matter. As Whitney (1993) suggests, decisions *about* education are one thing, and can be and have been overturned if children are not consulted. Decisions *within* education are quite different.

> Children have few rights at school. They have no right to see their personal files until they are 16 and even then few schools seem to make the facility available, so they have little opportunity to challenge what others have said about them. They cannot appeal in their own right against their exclusion; they are dependent on their parents doing so. Even then they have no automatic right to be present at any hearing, which may also not include any 'independent' person to represent their views. Whitney, 1993)

This restriction (Education (No 2) Act, 1986, section 26) is in sharp contrast to the 'Gillick Ruling in the same year which established that even a child under 16 is able to seek medical advice (e.g. for contraception) without parental consent, provided that she 'is of sufficient understanding to comprehend the advice which is given to her and the implications of it' (Feldman, 1993, p. 152.) As far as school management is concerned, 'children seem to be expected to accept the school rules with little opportunity for negotiation in the light of their individual circumstances or risk exclusion on the ground that they have broken the "contract of admission" on which their place was offered'. (Whitney, 1993, p.128). Further, the ban in section 15 of the 1986 Education Act on participation on governing bodies by individuals under 18 makes it impossible for young people at school to participate actively in formal educational decision making. Bastiani and Doyle (1994), in a publication for the National Consumer Council, recommend the removal of this prohibition which restricts the most obvious way in which school pupils can advocate for themselves and their peers. The conflict between this restriction and the apparent recognition of children's roles in decision making in *Choice and Diversity* (DES, 1992) is noted by these authors.

Some legislation which affects children in education appears to extend beyond the school walls. Pupils under the age of 12 are forbidden by the Education (No 2) Act, 1986 to engage in 'partisan political activities'. Feldman (1993) comments that 'there can be little serious doubt that the words of the (act) were intended to cover pursuit of such activities anywhere by registered pupils of the school, rather than merely while they are on school premises' (p. 571). As Feldman suggests, this restriction clearly breaches the European Convention on Human Rights and Article 13 of the UN Convention. At the very least it curtails debate and prevents children from exploring political ideas through role play in the classroom or elsewhere. The 1986 Act also forbids the promotion of partisan political views in schools, but as the same author points out, this has been breached only by the government itself, by the distribution of the 'Parents' Charter', which was objected to by some LEAs on the grounds that it represented the educational views of the Conservative Party.

The Education (Scotland) Act 1981 made formal provision for some parental rights to be transferred to young people at the age of 16, but the parallel 1981 Education Act made no such arrangements. However, Circular 1/83, which laid down the arrangements for statementing, did emphasise that '(t)he feelings and perceptions of the child concerned should be taken into account, and the concept of partnership should wherever possible be extended to older children and young persons'. Similarly, and rather surprisingly considering the interpolation of the 1989 Act between the two, the 1993 Act does not require such consultation about school placements or exclusions. With regard to the latter, children have no independent right to appeal until aged 18. The Code of Practice (1994) however, which it must be remembered is 'non statutory guidance' to which Local Authorities must 'have regard' in carrying out their statutory responsibilities, does make reference to consultation with children which is couched in similar terms to the 1989 Act. However, the Draft Regulations for the conduct of Special Educational Needs Tribunals state that although 'the Tribunal may wish to take account of the ascertainable views of the child and, on occasions, hear evidence from the child, (i)t will normally only seek evidence from the child with the parents' consent'. The 1989 Act thus stands out from the rest in philosophy and focus on the needs and wishes of the child. Whitney comments, 'There appears...to be some embarrassment that such a humane and enlightened piece of legislation may have slipped through unnoticed and a very real risk that it may not have the impact which was intended' (Whitney,

1993, p. 131). At the time of writing, the government is attempting to retrieve confidence in its concern for disability rights following the failure of the Civil Rights (Disabled Persons) Bill by the publication of a consultation document providing for a more limited range of rights. Interestingly these do not include the right of access to educational establishments.

The idea of advocacy, and the need for self-advocacy are thus promoted by international law and by one specific piece of British legislation. Within educational law, however, it appears that the child is still seen as the creature of his or her parents, and there is only limited opportunity for self-advocacy. The assumption remains that the wishes and interests of the child with regard to the conduct of his or her education are similar in all ways to those of the parents and that the child can be well represented by them. The whole issue of the rights of children is subordinated to the rights of the parents and of the educational establishments, to make decisions on their behalf.

Confused inputs, confused outcomes

Socially and educationally the piecemeal development of human rights legislation for adults or children in a country without a written constitution is confusing and paradoxical. It has meant that whereas individuals in 'minority' groups present issues of provision and participation in terms of human rights, legislators, bureaucrats and some support agencies see them as organisational problems. Thus they promote dependency, making sure that the 'needs' of the disabled are met, rather than recognising their rights to the same occupational, social and educational faciilities as the rest of the population. Beresford and Campbell (1994) consider that the providers of services and the recipients thereof have a different 'world view'; the first being 'preoccupied with services and people's relation to them as consumers, the latter are concerned with rights, empowerment and appropriate support to meet people's needs and maintain their independence'. Oliver (1990) describes some voluntary organisations as 'quite shameless' in the way they promote their clients as dependent recipients of charitable donations. (This is exemplified by the production of seriously disabled individuals accompanied by able-bodied 'minders' in some street collection campaigns.) Oliver argues that the 'professional and administrative' approach which permeates 'provision' reinforces this culture of dependency and the very term 'care' (as in 'community care') emphasises it. The individual's ability to chart a way through has traditionally depended on the quality of the advice received from the experts sought as advocates. In assessment for the statement of SEN, the parent offering a view is often encouraged to seek the advice of an independent educational psychologist, who will assemble arguments for the desired placement in the language best understood by the providers. The more a person is able to access and comprehend such advice, the better the deal he or she will get from the bureaucrats, but the less articulate, the less pressing, and the less confident find it harder to find a way through the maze, and are more likely to accept whatever is offered.

Several authors, including Bewley and Glendinning (1994) have recently questioned the adequacy and appropriateness of such representation, even where, within its own terms, it appears successful. They ask whether advocacy is enough: perhaps only the disabled individual can adequately represent his or her own interests, for only he or she will properly do so as a matter of human rights rather than effective consumerism. Where providers attempt to involve the disabled in planning groups, they argue, it is done haphazardly, often involving one or two token individuals who are expected to represent 'the disabled' as interested consumers, who must argue for a 'share of the cake'. Bewley and Glendinning noted that one community care project team was actually chaired by a disabled Social Services Officer who was described by a health authority manager as 'represent(ing) consumer views admirably'. For people in such a position to argue in terms of rights and equity would be seen as threatening established purchaser-provider relationships.

Can we extrapolate from the structure of provision for and representation of disabled individuals in the community at large to the situation of children, especially children with SEN in schools? It is arguable that we can. In each case, the 'consumers' (in this case the children) are divided into the competent, who can access the services (i.e. make subject choices), develop positive social relationships (avoid bullying), engage effectively with providers (are popular with staff) and are perceived as responsible, self -directed learners (reach the sixth form and are made prefects), and those others who do none of these thngs.   Oliver (1990) writes that the professional-client relationship is dependency creating, and even when the medical model of disability is replaced by an educational one, the identification of the teacher as the fount of all knowledge and distributor of privileges is itself disabling to those who do not hope to share in that fortune. Oliver goes on to compare the definition of independence offered by health care professionals 'in terms of self-care activities such as washing, dressing, toiletting, cooking and eating without assistance. Disabled people, however, define independence differently, seeing it as the ability to be in control of and make decisions about one's life, rather than doing things alone or without help' (Oliver, 1990, p. 91). Analogously, how often do we see the help offered to children with SEN couched in terms only of 'basic skills' or using public transport and filling in forms, rather than in understanding the franchise or dealing coherently with service agencies? Of course we cannot simply say that 'basic skills' are irrelevant, any more than even Oliver would regard the management of a toothbrush irrelevant, but they are not the only skills that should be part of the curriculum.

Oliver further comments on the way dependency is promoted by the experiences of the child with learning difficulties in school. They also see themselves as pitiful because they are socialised into accepting disability as a tragedy personal to them. This occurs because teachers like other professionals also hold to this view of disability, curriculum materials portray disabled people (if they appear at all) as pathetic victims or arch villains' (Oliver, 1990, p.92). From a recent study (Sandow, 1995, in press) it is clear that this view is transmitted to children, too. Asked to draw pictures of people who were clever, stupid, nice or nasty, 9 and 10 year olds consistently produced drawings which portrayed the 'stupid' as pathetic weedy frightened figures, and the 'nasty' as aggressive villainous ones.

Human rights have been identified as a vital issue in education (Lister, 1991). But they are not only relevant in the context of helping pupils to understand worldwide socio-political matters; they are also relevant in helping pupils to identify their *own* needs and capacities in the society in which they find *themselves*. This cannot be done purely as a matter of process: as Lister points out, '(t)here is a challenge for modern educators to identify *content* for the curriculum'. Lister seeks to persuade teachers to address the big issue of human rights through the individual experiences of children, 'to start from the people, the situations and the stories and then to build up analytical frameworks...to facilitate the analysis of human rights issues' (Lister, 1991, p. 246). In Chapters 2.2 and 2.3 of this book, some of the ways in which this process may be begun, and some curriculum content which may be useful, are identified. The challenge for teachers is therefore to address the issue of education about human rights in a way which is personally enabling for their pupils.

Chapter 1.2

DILEMMAS FOR ADVOCACY AND SELF-ADVOCACY

This chapter will outline some of the problems, both philosophical and practical, which surround advocacy and self-advocacy. These affect the legislator, the teacher, the parent.and the child. In aligning ourselves with those who would promote self-advocacy, we need to be aware that advocacy is not a simple process and cannot be encouraged simplistically.

What's in it for the advocate?

Our society has traditionally relied upon advocates. Certain individuals have become identified or have identified themselves as effective and necessary advocates. In the past, we needed advocates because traditionally, ordinary people could not read or write, and did not enter the charmed circle of the literate, who included the lawyer the teacher and the priest. These three were necessary to intervene or plead for the ignorant. Chaucer's pardoner was one of these. Some argue that today's advocates are as self-seeking as the pardoner. Wolfensberger (1989) for example suggests that whereas

> human services have traditionally been interpreted as moral enterprises of great positive impact on those on whom they are bestowed.....one can point to any number of instances where a human service was initiated or at leat funded primarily in order to serve the latent function of bringing glory and recogniton to a funder or donor rather than to serve the manifest function of serving its clients. (Wolfensberger, (1989, p. 27)

Even where the advocate believes himself to be disinterested, it is undeniable that the very existence of the client keeps him (the advocate) in a job. Thus advocacy itself relies on continued dependency for its existence, and according to Wolfensberger, must seek to create further dependents among the poor and dispossessed in order to retain its own legitimacy.

The genre reaches its most sophisticated form in the legal advocate. This is a person who has particular knowledge of a system which has enormous power over the lives of individuals and of which most people are in awe. While it is possible to dispense with the lawyer, the ordinary citizen is strongly dissuaded from doing so. Even in situations where a lawyer is specifically not required, such as the Industrial Tribunal, or even conveyancing, it is customary to employ one, as the assumption is that advocacy is essential. So also with the doctor, who will speak to the surgeon on behalf of the patient, or the priest who will intercede on the part of the sinner. Such advocates are still sought by those wishing to apply for a passport, even though another 'ordinary' person will do. We perceive ourselves as being less worthy of a hearing, a pardon, a consideration, or the right to travel abroad, unless someone speaks for us.

The complexity of the law and the procedures for making statements are a fertile field for the advocate. Few parents will contemplate fighting their own way through the system without an advocate. At the same time the assumption is that the 'street level bureaucrats' (Weatherley and Lipsky, 1977) are enemies, whose task is to prevent the disbursement of funds or assistance if possible. Recently, in one London Borough, attempts to set up a parent support system using available Education Support Grant (ESG) funds were treated with deep suspicion by local parents who believed that a person appointed by the LEA, whatever the job description, could not possibly act independently of the employer.

Working oneself out of a job

Professional involvement in special needs, as much as in these other fields, carries the danger that those teachers involved are equally dependent upon the existence of the clientele. The 'special needs industry' (Tomlinson, 1982) operates through a combination of the protocols and vested interests of teachers and administrators. This kind of advocacy is flawed, as it prevents self-advocacy for the client group whilst serving the latent interest of the provider. The only way to avoid the taint of self-interest is for the advocate to work seriously to deprive him or herself of a job. So the lawyer must teach the skills of self-presentation to the client, the priest reject the concept of intercession and the doctor allow the patient into his or her secrets. Teachers, similarly, must work to enable their students to do without them, but this presents professional difficulties of its own as shall be seen below. Social workers have recognised the dilemma, and are promoting the concept of 'empowerment'. However, it may be that empowerment itself is a new job, which does not in the final analysis disempower *the advocate*, but merely adds to the list of professional skills. The current enthusiasm for distance learning, begun by the Open University as a means of cheap mass higher education and now often encouraged for financial reasons by other institutions, is a case in point. Distance learning does not require less teaching, but does require different skills which at first are viewed with suspicion by those accustomed to working in more traditional ways.

The credibility of the advocate

Inasmuch as teachers have always seen themselves as advocates for their pupils, teachers in the special needs field have tended to adopt this role more than most. They have argued for services, facilities and staff; they have promoted their pupils' skills to parents; they have attempted to protect them from rejection; they have sought work placements and recreational opportunities. Unfortunately they have been handicapped by the low esteem in which they have been held by other teachers and by managers and administrators (Sandow and Garner, 1994). One way in which their advocacy has been reduced in effectiveness has been to direct it into safe but low level activities such as fund raising, and by delineating the curriculum as a series of time-consuming tasks which are therapeutic, occupational but not enabling. Staff in special needs departments sometimes feel the need to legitimate their existence by taking on some respected academic subject work as well. In addition, their influence is often constrained by the physical placement of the 'Unit' at the other side of the playground, thereby confirming to others the separateness of their role: *'here comes the sanctuary man'*, *'You and your special needs kids'* . Sometimes they have also felt frustrated by parents' wishes to direct their children's energies into a restricted curriculum in the search for the basic skills perceived as so important in employment.

The position of the child in the educational system

The nature and function of childhood has changed over centuries, as described by Aries (1962). For most of the time that education has been compulsory, teaching has been characterised by despotism, of a more or less benign kind. Parents have seen teachers as the means by which knowledge and social skills were 'instilled' into their children, the more the better. Traditionally, the idea that children should participate in the learning process, other than in the rehearsing of facts and the completion of exercises, was relatively unacknowledged. Alternative educational formulae have been seen as at best odd, and at worst distinctly subversive. At the classroom desk, as at the dining room table at home, children were supposed to be seen and not heard. Child-centred education, discussed in more detail in the next chapter, changed this. The roles of teacher and child were fused as it was recognised that teachers learned from children how best to teach. By working with children, teachers were able to perceive more clearly how the learning process developed, and this was even more revealing where children appeared to show difficulties in learning. So child-centredness was as much about how teachers taught as about how children learned. If the teacher becomes a facilitator, rather than an instructor, the child becomes a self-directed learner, and therefore a participant rather than a recipient.

Participation is intended to be enabling; to free the child from the need always to ask for permission to learn. The child must and will speak for herself, which is where self-advocacy begins for the majority. However, for those for whom learning is more of a challenge, the focus has been on the imparting of skills and knowledge, and the method has been instrumental and didactic. In the 1960s, while Plowden reigned in the ordinary school, in special education the analogy of the bucket to be filled was quoted with approval by the behavioural gurus of the day.

Unsuitable for some?

So are there some for whom self-advocacy is unsuitable? Self-advocacy presupposes that rational decisions can be made by all including those with learning difficulties. Society commonly takes the view that there are some who do not deserve, and some who cannot take advantage of, ordinary human rights. Children who are 'disruptive' and are identified as having emotional or behavioural difficulties (EBD) are considered to have forsaken their right to debate either the educational or social outcomes of their time in school. 'I'd lock the door and throw away the key' is a common enough response to murderers, rapists or other perpetrators of serious crimes. This is the case even where very young children are involved; the parents of Jamie Bulger collected huge numbers of signatures for their petition that Thompson and Venables should *never* be released. In education, exclusion from school has become permanent for an increasing number of adolescents who have incurred the displeasure of adults.

In the area of severe learning difficulties (SLD), the extension of voting rights, and the availability of sex education are still controversial. Those with SLD are perceived as too vulnerable to make decisions about their lives, and the decisions they can take, for instance about using public transport or initiating personal relationships, are heavily circumscribed. Although in recent years the cognitive level at which such assumptions are made has been lowered, there still remain instances of treatment without consent which infringe the individual rights of the child. In the case of the child with SLD as well as the one with EBD, the individual is seen as a potential threat to society. The dilemma for the teacher is thus to decide whether to extend to such children the same rights to self-representation as are afforded to others, or whether to act instead as a guardian, protecting the child from the world and the world from the child. In doing so, the teacher may have to contend with the anxieties of parents as well as the concerns of officials.

Should self-advocacy be age-related?

'Act your age'
'If you behave like an adult I'll treat you like an adult'
'Don't be a baby'
'You're old enough to know better'..

Implicit in these clichés is the belief that rights and responsibilities are age-related. Moral psychologists like Kohlberg and Erickson as well as Piaget and Freud have instilled in us that stages of development are age-related. These philosophies have been adapted to fulfil this age's view of the duration and nature of childhood. Thus an incremental giving of responsibility begins with the awarding of pocket money, and the entrusting of errands, but it is only recently, in tthe 1989 Children Act (and following that, in the Code of Practice that follows from the 1993 Act) that children are required to be consulted 'in accordance with their age and experience' about their views regarding where and with whom they shall live, or how they shall be educated. On the whole, young children are perceived as relatively incompetent in judgement: only after age 8 are children assumed to be able to understand the difference between right and wrong and the age of formal criminal responsibility is 10 Above this age however, anomalies abound: The age for military service is 17 although the age for the vote is 18, the age for marriage is 16 but the age for legal homosexual relations is 18. Taken individually, all of these constraints may be justifiable, but they remain contradictory. They also take no cognisance of individual differences, and have the effect of morally segregating children from adults. It apears we cannot make our minds up about when or whether an individual should take responsibility for his or her life, and in what respect. The education system has many explicit and inferred rules concerning age-appropriateness. Thematic approaches prevail in the primary school, but subject-based teaching operates in the secondary school. At 14, children are expected to make 'choices' about their subject specialism, but from a list which may be based more on pragmatism than logic. (In the case of the learning disabled child, the choices are even more circumscribed.) Sixth-formers are alone entitled to a 'common-room' . All these represent rites of passage: but they are amazingly haphazard. Compared with earlier generations, children today are given fewer responsibilities, and maybe fewer rights. Childhood has been extended with the school leaving age.

However, as the High Scope project has demonstrated, even children of nursery age are able to engage in decision making about their own curriculum and appear to profit from it (Hohman et al, 1979). This is sadly contrasted with the increasing emphasis on protection and stranger-anxiety which means that the current generation of primary school children rarely even take responsibility for getting themselves to and from school alone. So the dilemma here is for parents, teachers and legislators: should we lower the age at which we begin to listen to children's views and allow them rights, even at the cost of exposing them to external dangers and the risk of failure, or raise it in order to protect them as long as possible? And is it logical to accept different 'ages of consent' for different functions?

Self-advocacy as cruelty

Empowerment requires that someone can recognise that they lack power, as defined by the professional. But the kinds of power advocated by the professional, including social and personal independence, voting rights and earning power, may seem quite irrelevant to a particular individual living a very different life from the professional. Concomitantly, the individual is invited to accept the right of the professional to define power, and identify the occasions and places where it must be used; again the relevance of this may be questionable. They must be trained to use the words and skills of the advocate, usually by the advocate. Thus we find parents of disabled children talking about how they 'accept' the child (though they have never failed to love him or her) and those whose children are causing difficulties 'acknowledging the problem' instead of worrying about it. The professional urges and even requires them to be self-advocates whether they like it or not, and an inability to recognise the lack of power may be part of the problem as perceived from outside. So power, as defined by the professional, usually middle-class 'helper', may be irrelevant to the real needs of the individual. 'Community care' is a case in point. The responsibility 'given' to the discharged patient may not contribute to his or her happiness, or enable successful functioning in the outside world. The power to sit in a beach shelter all day, because the hostel is closed, may feel more like disenfranchisement. There is often a presumption that only the clever (and rich) have a right to power, and a tradition that 'ordinary people' should know their place. In school, children are socialised into a system where the high achiever is the one who has the right to answer the question, and those with special needs become accustomed to, and prefer, anonymity. In such a context it may be that to impose self-advocacy, by requiring contributions or involvement may result in embarrassment, or ridicule. The cure may be worse than the disease.

We must guard against assuming that children want to direct their own learning. Children have very fixed views about the role of schools and the teachers within them. Such views have developed through tradition, transmitted through parents, through comics, films and television, all of which reinforce stereotypical views of schools and teachers. Teachers in primary schools often reward pupils for completed work with the instruction to 'choose' something for themselves. This is not, however, always welcomed. When children in one school known to the writers were asked what they most disliked about school they replied, 'playtime' and 'choosing'.

Similarly, the current emphasis on parental 'choice' of school is based on the assumption that choice is what parents want, and that the choice will be based on academic factors. However, as Riddell *et al.* (1994) point out, working-class (sic) families may choose schools for quite other reasons, and may be blamed for so doing. Much has been written about the desirability of the 'internal locus of control' (ILC) and the supposed absence of this within the disadvantaged sections of society. However, an unpublished study (Rowe, 1993) suggested that contrary to expectation, highly disadvantaged students in a tuition centre for young people in care demonstrated both an ILC similar to high achieving controls, and considerable insight into their own difficulties. The focus of decision-making may be different from that promoted by professional advocates, but the activity is similar. The dilemma here is to promote self-confidence and the ability to act for oneself, while accepting that the goals of the pupil may not accord with one's own. In any case, not wishing to be a self-advocate is a choice in itself.

Is it fair?

In an age when education is a preparation for life in the workplace (or the dole queue) teachers and schools may be forgiven for thinking that independent thought and the ability to argue coherently a minority view may not be the skills best suited to long-term employment. In the workplace creative thinkers are not popular: perhaps they should not be encouraged at school? In particular, this may be a point argued by those teaching children with SEN, for they are most likely to be left without work. The joke about the dustman with the PhD is a bit too close to reality. If schools do not attempt to mirror the workplace, perhaps they are truly subversive. Professionals may quite like the idea of subversion (Harris, 1982) but they recognise that it may threaten their existence and certainly their independence. Since 1988 teachers have seen the gradual destruction of that independence, led by those who quite openly seek to restructure and incidentally to proletarianise their profession. The Teacher *Training* Agency was carefully named. There are other professional concerns.

Self-protection, structure and tradition in the professions

The continued existence of an occupation or craft depends on the maintenance and ownership of discrete skills. When those skills are given away as when the joiner teaches the amateur how to produce acceptable woodwork, the craft is threatened. As with carpentry, so with teaching. In the 1960s when parents were actively discouraged from teaching their children to read, the anxieties about 'reading readiness' obscured the professionals' sense of threat that a special skill was being taken from them. But as Barbara Tizard once remarked, 'there is nothing special about teaching reading. Children were taught from the Bible long before there were reading schemes'.

Allowing people to make mistakes is a threat to professional skills. This is so especially where the process is observed: a teacher faced with an OFSTED inspector will feel particularly threatened if mistakes are made. Self-advocacy and its processes can also be seen as threats to order and tradition: an excess of democracy which operates against the preservation of the system. The William Tyndale affair is only one example often cited in support of this view. Self-advocacy is thus unlikely to be popular in a traditional staffroom.This may be why the provision of opportunities for children to give their side of the story does not mean that such accounts will automatically be given status. Self-advocacy is threatening. Hence the criticism by many children (Garner, 1993a) that they are allowed to discuss things in a 'school council', but that their recommendations are seldom taken into account, or that the decisions they are allowed to make are trivial and inconsequential compared to those which are made for them. There are ways in which such processes can be made effective, however, as shown in Chapter 2.3.

Do student teachers need to worry about this?

It may be argued that student teachers and newly qualified teachers (NQTs) have quite enough to worry about without saddling them with issues of advocacy and self-advocacy. Basic skills, lesson planning, self-evaluation may all seem more immediate needs. It is worth however, thinking about the learning process experienced by these selfsame students: they have to learn to think and speak for themselves, and not simply to absorb the view of the profession promoted by their teachers, whether in colleges or in schools. The same is true of their own pupils. Observing the way in which their tutors deal with dissent or criticism will be part of their training. In addition, students need to learn how to respect their pupils as individuals and not to see them as opponents in some kind of battleground, as suggested by some texts (see for example Smith and Laslett, 1993). It is unfortunate if NQTs begin their careers having absorbed a siege mentality; they are unlikely to be able to empathise with their pupils if they do so. On the other hand it may be that only with the confidence of experience can young teachers begin to allow pupils a voice. Asking awkward questions can be a threat to the well-planned lesson. Student teachers are desperate for everything to go perfectly the first time, especially if observed. This is an issue not only for students and NQTs but for their mentors. Evaluation and discussion of a lesson can take account of relationships and responses as well as inputs and outcomes.

Providing the tools for self-advocacy

Within the field of SLD teaching, and to some extent in MLD and EBD schools, the development of behavioural approaches to teaching has undeniably opened up new horizons for the most difficult and disabled children (Ainscow and Tweddle, 1979; Westmacott and Cameron, 1984). However, such methods may seem far removed from the facilitatory style which seems to lead to participation and self-advocacy. Teachers in special schools would be loath to abandon the methods which they observe have enabled children with most severe problems to participate in social and cognitive activities. Such teachers would point to the failure of 'discovery methods' to engage the attention of such pupils, and to the real advances in self-control and self-management which have resulted from behavioural pedagogy and the detailed task analysis which has accompanied it. Such methods have been criticised precisely because they appear to deny the free will of the child, and to render him or her a pawn in the hands of the teacher. The best behavioural programmers have recognised the importance of involving the child in the selection of goals and of the programme of reinforcement. In fact, programmes which do not engage the subject in this way often founder when attempts are made to generalise the newly learned skill to other environments. However, at very basic levels, learning programmes depend at the start on very simple rules for inhibiting undesired and initiating desired behaviour by the operation of reinforcement schedules which are outside the control of the child. The teacher must decide whether such overt manipulation is ethical if the end justifies the means.

An issue for institutional concern?

In an educational system which is market-oriented, SEN providers must fight for their customers against the competing interest of other sections of the education system for space, facilities, staff and status. Thus instead of collaboration, the competitive ethos takes over. The focus of that competition is defined in academic terms, with particular reference to the National Curriculum (NC). Teachers already complain that the exigencies of the NC mean that not enough time is left to teach basic skills like reading; how can they find time for activities which can be seen as time-consuming 'frills'? For a while it appeared that the inclusion of 'speaking and listening' provided opportunities for the promotion of self-advocacy, but recently the downgrading of this, and of activities like drama and music, to say nothing of the failure to include a foreign language in the primary school curriculum, have all combined to reduce opportunities for promoting self-advocacy in the classroom. (Chapters 2.2 and 2.3 demonstrate how valuable such activities can be.)

Conclusion

We have identified here just a few of the dilemmas which face us when attempting to promote self-advocacy. Every innovator is faced with those who prefer to continue to do things in traditional ways. Nevertheless, there are ways of moving forward, and good reasons for doing so, as the next sections will show.

Chapter 1.3

THE POTENTIAL OF ADVOCACY AND SELF-ADVOCACY

This chapter will suggest that including the views of children has highly practical benefits for all pupils, but especially those who have SEN. It will also project its potential for whole schools and the teachers within them. Reference will be made to a number of historical precedents for the promotion of the role of the child in educational decision making. At various points in this book it is noted that, in the wake of fifteen or so years of change in the organisation of education (Arnot and Barton, 1992), this has been largely overshadowed. But, combined with more recent adaptations of these ideas in the context of SEN, they exemplify the benefits of 'inclusive' approaches which allow children a voice.

The tradition of liberal, child-centred education has been a colourful one. It has been unfairly criticised as a mainly philosophical approach, whose practical implications are open to question. This chapter revisits some of them, as a starting point to validate the strategies for pupil-involvement. These approaches can be traced in the history of education in both Europe and North America. Some recent examples of 'cooperative decision making' which appear to continue this tradition are also described. They show that, even in a period when 'pupils with special educational needs are not viewed as politically significant and questions of social justice and equity become marginalised' (Barton and Oliver, 1992), pupil-participation is workable and a potent means of securing equality of opportunity.

Lessons from history: the international legacy

Enlightened teaching, wherein the teacher perceives the child as a partner in an interactive effort to promote knowledge and uncover understanding, has a remarkable tradition in general education (Darling, 1994). It is hardly surprising therefore that recent governments in England have seen it as both contradictory and threatening to a newly formulated market-driven philosophy in education. Educational administrators, whose work is now framed by the need to provide value for money in a system governed by the scientific laws of economics and the desire to exercise control via statutory arrangements, have been the first to feel threatened by the 'progressive' view that individuals are not inanimate, unthinking receptacles into which facts are poured. Alongside this some practitioners assert that the 'children are ineducable and mainly in need of care' (Wallwork, 1990) whilst some approaches, notably therapeutiic interventions with those who have emotional and behavioural difficulties (EBD) are regarded with great suspicion. In consequence, their defence mechanism operates via a series of well-publicised, if largely unsubstantiated, attacks on what they regard as 'do-gooders' in education (Lawlor, 1990).

The legacy of child-centredness has recently been in danger of becoming lost amidst instrumentalist demands fuelled by such political dogma and criticism. At the outset, therefore, this progressive tradition needs to be re-emphasised and its efficacy for the 1990s confirmed. A widespread view was that *all* who participate in a child-centred approach to teaching and learning can benefit. Although we cannot provide an exhaustive historical review of these movements, the net can be cast widely. Such historical developments, not only in England but also in mainland Europe and North America, helped to support the idea that children should have a far more significant role in schools than that allowed by the educational mandarins of the present day.

Comenius, in the 17th century, wrote of schools that 'they are the terror of boys and the slaughter houses of minds...where what ought to be poured in gently is violently forced in and beaten in'. He proposed that 'common schools' should be established, in which equal opportunities to learn would be provided through a 'humane treatment of pupils'. He also stated that 'if the pupil does not learn readily, this is the fault of no-one but the teacher, who either does not know how to make his pupil receptive of knowledge or does not take the trouble to do so'.

Rousseau provides a further early illustration of the type of liberal education being proposed by Comenius. A central theme of his educational writing was that children should be encouraged to participate as equal partners in learning. The importance of the child as an active learner was succinctly expressed with Rousseau's affirmation that 'Childhood has its own way of seeing, thinking and feeling'.

Rousseau's writings subsequently influenced Pestalozzi and Froebel, who argued that the child should be free to experiment, to learn by doing, free from the overbearing 'control' of the teacher. What each of these writers was implying was that teachers should, above all, provide the opportunity for children to gain access to learning by intuitive means, and that an important strategy to promote this was a 'freedom to learn'. Froebel argued that formal education systems 'go on stamping our children like coins'. The inference was that little opportunity was provided for individualism. The beliefs espoused by Rousseau, Pestalozzi and others was that children should be given the opportunity to learn by understanding and involvement. This bears a close parallel to the framework which many teachers have sought to provide to enable the growth of advocacy and self-advocacy in contemporary schools and classrooms.

Finally, it may be noted that Dewey too subscribed to these views. He regarded children as active participants in the learning process rather than passive recipients of what the teacher had to offer. In particular he stressed shared activity, wherein '(a) spirit of free communication, of interchange of ideas, suggestions, results...becomes the dominating note'.

The ideas promoted by these and other writers had a profound effect on the way in which education was organised in England. Their impact was especially noticeable because the English education system has always been less receptive to new ideas. Practitioners joined with theorists in establishing the New Education Fellowship, which sought to advance child-centred approaches in preference to more traditional, hierarchical teaching. Campbell (1938), provided a succinct statement of their general intent, suggesting that 'It is not what we do to the child or for the child that educates him, but what we enable him to do for himself, to see and learn and feel and understand for himself' (p.83).

Several themes enshrined in the kinds of child-centred approaches described above, contribute to the legitimation of advocacy and self-advocacy in the work that teachers do with children who have SEN. Amongst these are the beliefs that:

- all children learn best by experience;
- a teacher's role is to provide opportunities for these experiences to be developed;
- in order that such opportunities are promoted the child should be viewed as an equal partner in the learning
- communication with the child is essential to realise the first three

Each of these principles became the focus of considerable debate, the argument being characterised as one between 'traditional' and 'progressive' values. This reached its climax in the 1960s and 1970s.

Progressive education: Plowden and post-Plowden

The Plowden Report (DES, 1967) is an appropriate starting point for a *résumé* of more recent developments in England of child-centred teaching and learning. The Report represented a landmark in the development of a 'new' child-centredness in English education (Darling, 1994). The period also coincided with an era in England when provision for those children who had SEN was coming under considerable scrutiny. The Warnock Committee marked a culmination of this interest. To many, therefore, the era became synonymous with a more 'progressive' form of special education.

An influential factor in these events was a noticeable change in outlook promoted by the effects of political and social conditions of the late 1960s. There was a newly established belief in the primacy of individual freedom, and a consequent move to establish an educational philosophy which enabled every child to be seen in his or her own, individual frame of reference. These ideas did not go unchallenged and the period was also marked by a series of much-publicised debates which highlighted the contrasting belief-systems of the opposing camps (Cox and Dyson, 1969; Peters, 1969).

The Plowden Report represented a landmark in the movement for child-centred learning. It gave a profound impetus to individualised teaching in which the child, rather than a given curriculum subject, was viewed as the focus for development. Many of the Plowden proposals were viewed as revolutionary, demanding changes in attitude and understanding by teachers and significant alterations to the way in which schools and classrooms were organised. As Rogers (1980) summarised, 'teachers had to adapt their methods to individuals in a class. Only in that way could the needs of gifted and slow-learning children...be met' (p.84).

More particularly, the Report emphasised two themes, both previously overlooked, which would have an important bearing on developing advocacy and self-advocacy in SEN. Firstly, Plowden noted that educational disadvantage was a significant factor in underachievement. It recommended positive discrimination in the way in which educational resources were distributed, advocating the establishment of 'educational priority areas' (EPAs). Additionally, the Report stressed the importance of the role of parents in the education of their children. It emphasised that schools should provide greater opportunities for them to discuss the progress of their children. In both cases, important principles of advocacy and self-advocacy were being established which would subsequently be developed in SEN practice. Finally, it is worth acknowledging that Plowden gave consideration to the way in which children who had SEN in ordinary schools were educated, thereby signalling the forthcoming movement for integration.

The Plowden Report had an immense effect. Its influence on teacher education, on home-school relationships, on classroom organisation and upon teaching and learning styles became a dominant feature of the educational landscape of the 1970s. Several educationists began to promote child-centred approaches. It was an opportune time to do so. Not only was the social and political climate right, but a new group of influential writers were beginning to amplify the spirit of the Report: Neill, Freire, Holt, Illich, Dearden and Peters amongst them.

During the same period another set of ideas began to influence educational thinking. Community education developed in the 1960s, influenced significantly by events in the United States and by the global movement to 'de-school'. The crux of community school philosophy was that formal education had become divorced from the needs of its recipients.and that teachers and administrators held beliefs and values which were removed from those of pupils and the wider society.

The influence of progressive educationists, including the supporters of community education, was marked. In order to provide effective education in a rapidly changing world, schools needed to respond by taking notice of the cultural differences which were becoming increasingly evident in post-industrial societies. Remarkable amongst the protagonists of this approach was Illich (1973), who stated that 'schools are unworldly, and make the world non-educational', and that 'they discourage the poor from taking control of their own learning'. He argued that 'An illusion on which the school system rests is that most learning is the result of teaching'.

Underpinning much of this thinking was the belief that schools, far from being places which support or promote equality, are places in which inequality is legitimised. As with child-centredness, this form of progressivism was met with considerable criticism, especially because it challenged the existing hierarchical order of education systems in the post-industrial world. This criticism came from two sources. On the one hand there were those who believed that schools can do very little to promote or sustain equality because factors *outside* schools (access to employment, health and welfare services, adequate housing, party-political dogma) dictated arrangements within them. Little could be gained, therefore, by making schools into more democratic institutions.

On the other hand, right-wing thinkers, politicans and economists believed that the existing 'balance', between rich and poor, or between able and disabled, needed to be maintained in order to preserve capitalist economies. As Lister (1972) has observed, 'Education is the mass service industry of modern society. It creates the need for its own products, and it validates its own activities' (p. 7). In SEN, for instance, this debate can be exemplified by the arguments for a vocational, as opposed to a liberal, curriculum (Dyson, 1985; Galletley, 1985).

The potential of recent initiatives in special educational needs

The Warnock Report (DES, 1978) gave a hint of the potential for incorporating the views of the child who has SEN within both the decision-making frameworks which concerned them and the more general, day-to-day educational experiences from which hitherto they had been excluded. An overt statement of the possibilities for the child (and the teacher) was contained in the multidisciplinary approach recommended by Warnock, wherein all participants have a crucial input in order to resolve the learning difficulties.

It could be argued that Warnock promised rather more than it delivered. Certainly by the time that its main recommendations were included in the Education Act of 1981, there began to be an uneasy feeling that legislative rhetoric held precedence over practical outcomes where the question of advocacy and self-advocacy was concerned. But that is another, more depressing, story.

The last ten or fifteen years have witnessed a number of initiatives in SEN which draw upon the ideas from the progressive legacy outlined above. Although small in number, they none the less show that when pupils are directly involved in planning, policy development and evaluation in schools, there are significant benefits for everyone involved. These may be regarded as the immediate predecessors of a new awareness of the merits of progressive, child-centred practice in SEN teaching. The benefits have been summarised by Davie (1993): 'involving children and young people in decision-making will, if sustained and developed, lead to a more 'holistic' professional perspective' (p. 145).

In SEN a precursor of this kind of approach was provided by a small number of special schools which operated along what can be generalised as 'therapeutic' lines (Galloway *et al.*, 1982). Often these were schools for children who had EBD. Many promoted individual rights of pupils by offering opportunities for children to be included in the decision-making machinery of the school. Frequently this was supported by psychotherapy (Cornish and Clarke, 1975). Cooper (1993), in a review of the efficacy of 'learning from pupils perspectives', articulates the importance of humanistic, child-centred approaches in a contemporary context, stating that

> An underlying principle shared by these approaches is that emotional and behavioural difficulties are often embedded in the ways in which individuals perceive themselves and their environment...In these circumstances emotional and behavioural change stems from the articulation and analysis of these perceptions (p. 129)

During the last twenty years there has developed a small, but important body of literature concerning the benefits of listening to the views of children in both mainstream and special schools. This material has been important for both philosophical and practical reasons. In the first case, it has been essential to maintain a bridgehead of advocacy and self-advocacy at a time when education in general, and SEN in particular, has become increasingly market-led, with the commensurate reduction in opportunities to secure pupil-entitlement: local management of schools (LMS), for example, has significantly weakened LEA support-services (NUT, 1993), traditionally an important means of advocacy for children who have SEN.

The literature also contained an increasing amount of practical evidence that classrooms and schools are able to function far more effectively when children are given opportunities to be involved in decision-making (Furtwengler, 1989; Garner, 1992; Reynolds, 1985; Stevenson, 1991). This is crucial if teachers are to be convinced that it is worthwhile for them to change their style of teaching so that pupils with SEN can participate more fully in their own learning. What has been particularly encouraging is that an increasing amount of this kind of literature has been devoted to children who have EBD, previously that group of SEN pupils who were most disenfranchised (Schostak, 1983). These examples have shown that teachers can achieve considerable success, and personal fulfilment, by adopting a negotiating approach in the classroom. Together with the historical legacy of child-centredness in general education, they provide a platform for further developments in this aspect of SEN work.

The potential in a contemporary context

The legacy of child-centredness, whether in mainstream education or generic special education, provides a means of validating its extended use in SEN, by actively promoting advocacy and self-advocacy. Arguments for the resulting participation of pupils and parents in all aspects of educational decision making, have to provide responses to the dilemmas we have presented in the previous chapter. Whilst it is probably the case that many of those working in SEN maintain a strong commitment to the rights of individual children, such personal belief-systems need to provide evidence that pupil participation is justifiable. This needs to be done on both philosophical and practical grounds, as a riposte to those who argue for schools structured on traditionalist working practices ('back to basics'?). At least three benefits of increased pupil participation can be identified, thereby outlining the potential for extending this way of working.

Benefits for the Child

Children who have learning difficulties respond well to cooperative teaching and learning strategies. From a whole-school perspective these approaches may be developed by providing the necessary climate in which children feel that they have a direct input into the organisation of the curriculum. Whilst the impact of the National Curriculum may have restricted the opportunities for decision making regarding specific content, there are none the less several strategies leading towards 'inclusivity' which may generate such participation. Some of these have been promoted in the official literature on curriculum differentiation and on the role of the child in identification and assessment.

Much has been made in the last ten years or so of derivatives of collaborative learning. Publicity given to the success of paired-reading schemes, peer-tutoring and group-work means that the validity of shared learning experiences has been widely established. The rate at which children who have learning difficulties progress in these learning situations helps to confirm a view that extending this participatory practice to include teacher-pupil collaboration may have an equally dramatic effect on pupil performance.

Studies which have sought the views of children who have SEN give some indications in support of shared learning strategies, whether it be in planning content, defining the preferred way in which lessons are taught, or in evaluating classroom performance.

Recent official publications have amplified the importance of pupil involvement in curriculum matters. The SEN Code of Practice (DfE, 1994a), for example, in defining the nature of pupil participation, suggests that 'The effectiveness of any assessment and intervention will be influenced by the involvement and interest of the child or young person concerned' (p. 14). The official view is now that curriculum intervention will not be successful unless the child has an input: 'their support is crucial to the effective implementation of any individual education programmes' (p. 14).

Individual Education Plans (IEPs), according to practice in the United States, make the child the fulcrum around which all teaching and learning activity should take place. In the Code of Practice they are seen as a central feature of Stage 2 of identification and assessment. There is, however, only an implicit assumption that pupil *and* teacher are partners. None of the documentation concerning IEPs refers to the substantive involvement of pupils in planning curriculum intervention. This is a major weakness of the directive, showing that the Code contains substantial amounts of rhetoric which consequently litter the document with paradoxes. On the other hand, official recognition, however subliminally inferred, has been obtained, to suggest that children do benefit from shared decision making.

Cooperation with others also builds self-esteem. Children who have special needs frequently lack confidence, and this is often manifest in a reluctance to engage in learning tasks. Moreover, they are often unwilling to talk with teachers about their learning problems. Cooperative work with other children, whether peers or older pupils, has shown that they can make gains in self-assurance, resulting in more on-task behaviour and learning progress. Teachers who involve SEN pupils in curriculum planning have similarly noted an increased enthusiasm in lessons. Contact with significant adults, whether teacher, parent or other, in which the pupil feels s/he is treated with respect can assist in this development (Davis and Stubbs, 1989).

Many pupils, particularly those whose SEN are associated with so-called problem behaviour, have underdeveloped social skills (DfE, 1994a). Often this can lead them to misinterpret the actions of other children or adults and can lead to inappropriate behaviour. Working alongside teachers can be a means of providing a role-model for them so that the intricate social events and exchanges which accompany learning can be rationalised and understood by them. Joint planning of curriculum experiences may also increase the level of conceptual understanding by SEN pupils.

In the wider context of the school there is now gathering evidence that pupil participation in decision making can lead to a reduction in the alienation felt by many so-called 'disruptive' pupils. This has now been officially recognised. The Elton Report (DES, 1989) and the DfE Circular relating to 'problem pupils' (DfE, 1994d) imply that pupil participation is rather more than simply desirable. Circular 8/94, entitled 'Pupil Behaviour and Discipline', for instance, states that when a behaviour policy is being developed its contents 'should be worked out cooperatively' (p. 3).

Benefits for the Teacher

Working cooperatively with children, whether in developing policies, planning individual lesson content, or in refining disciplinary procedures, enables a teacher to extend the range of teaching styles in the classroom. Woods (1979) identified boredom in lessons as an important cause of problem behaviour. Elsewhere, Galloway et al.. (1982) have noted that mixed-ability grouping provides teachers with the opportunity to present curriculum material in innovative ways, so that pupils with SEN have more opportunity to succeed. As Topping (1992) has commented, 'It will be important that teachers see cooperative learning as an alternative and effective route to National Curriculum attainment targets, which can have the additional benefit of positive attitudinal and social side-effects'.

Much has recently been made of the need for teachers to provide pupils with a variety of learning experiences. OFSTED, 1993b). Searle (1994), commenting on the role of teachers who work with 'disruptive' pupils, has indicated that the demands placed upon them can often be used positively. If schools are encouraged not to exclude pupils with behaviour problems, the teachers have to develop innovatory teaching styles to ensure that lessons meet the learning needs of the disaffected. This, as Ingram and Worrall (1993) have indicated, can be done by fostering cooperative approaches in the curriculum. Pupils whose special needs are associated with behaviour problems frequently complain that they are excluded from decisions made on their behalf (Garner, 1993a, 1993c; Sheppard, 1988).

Pupil involvement can also provide teachers with an effective way of managing whole classrooms. The emphasis upon good classroom management skills has been identified both by OFSTED (1993b) and by CATE (1992) as being indicators of a 'good' teacher. Allowing pupils to take responsibility for some aspects of classroom management, including their involvement in discipline matters, provides teachers with another strategy to ensure good organisation. Moreover, in establishing cooperative routines the child who has SEN can be more effectively incorporated into the social life of the classroom.

The latter point is particularly important in the professional development of teachers. Whilst this will be considered in greater detail in the final chapter, it needs to be acknowledged that teaching is now viewed as comprising a set of competences which can be measured by inspection. Being an effective classroom teacher in these terms means that consideration should be given to ways in which children can 'manage their own learning' and become 'involved in the wider social life of the school'. An increase in pupil participation reflects well upon the teacher: status and career prospects may be consequently enhanced.

Benefits for the School

What is good for pupils and their teachers is also good for whole schools. Those schools which provide opportunities for pupils to share in decision making have been described as 'inclusive' (Reynolds, 1985). The climate or ethos which characterises this has been described as one where 'teachers treat pupils courteously, respect their ideas, value their individuality, and listen carefully to what they have to say' (DES, 1989). The official view is that this promotes a situation wherein pupils are 'much more likely to respect teachers and behave considerately and sensibly themselves' (DES, op. cit.).

If this is the case the benefits to the school are substantial. Moreover, official recognition that such a school is 'effective' may well be forthcoming. Part 4 of the current school inspection schedule (OFSTED, 1993) identifies a number of criteria on which such a judgement is based. Amongst these are 'the range of, and pupils' responses to, opportunities to exercise responsibility and initiative' (p. 21) and whether the overall quality of relationships is such that 'pupils feel free to express and explore their views openly and honestly, and are willing to listen to opinions which they may not share' (p. 16). Conversely, there is a recognition that a school may be providing unsatisfactory learning experiences where pupils 'demonstrate undue dependence on the teacher or uncritical use of resources. They are reluctant to take initiatives or accept responsibility' (p. 9).

An element of pragmatism in response to official judgements may also be applied when considering the whole-school's approach to children who have SEN. Hence, the same inspection schedule requires schools to demonstrate that pupils are able to work collaboratively and to 'encourage all pupils to contribute to school life and to exercise responsibilities' (p. 64). More specifically, for those pupils who have statements of SEN, inspectors will judge the quality of provision in part on the extent to which 'he or she participate(s) in the Annual Review' (p. 67).

In meeting these evaluation criteria a school will serve its own interests as well as those of the child. Several other benefits, of a less utilitarian but equally important nature, may ensue for those schools which increase the level of pupil participation. Enhanced participation is, according to Brandes and Ginnis (1990) a notable means by which schools can cope with the massive changes and increased statutory requirements demanded of them since 1988. They argue that 'Participation *in* management by those affected *by* management is a very effective "coping resource"' (p. 197). Teachers, including heads, who feel that policy matters and their practical implications are being shared as part of an extended team which includes children who have SEN, will tend to be insulated from the loneliness felt by decision makers (or decision receivers).

Participation may therefore be said to reduce stress levels within the whole school. Institutions which allow pupils to contribute to policy making, whether in the social or academic curriculum, tend to be those least characterised by confrontation between staff and pupils (Cronk, 1987). Opposition by pupils (and by certain teachers, for that matter) to the undemocratic way in which schools are organised and run, on the other hand, results in a high level of conflict, and resultant stress for all those involved (Adams, 1991).

Conclusion

Any strategy which ensures greater involvement of pupils, either in the formal taught curriculum or in the hidden, social curriculum, results in both specific and general educational dividends. Not only are the learning needs of a particular section of the school population more adequately addressed, but the performances of others in a classroom or whole school are enhanced. Ultimately, such individual actions and responses provide the bedrock upon which a school's ethos or climate is built. And this, according to many, is the arbitrator of what comprises an effective school for all.

The benefits need to be viewed on two contextual levels. In the first place, the increased participation of children who have SEN is now to be viewed as a right, to which all teachers should be working towards. No distinction should be made between categories of need, so that the old status hierarchies are finally dispensed with. In allowing for advocacy and self-advocacy practices, teachers must ensure that democracy is maintained not only *between* pupils with SEN but also *within* the overall group itself.

Furthermore, a rational response to recent DfE directives and OFSTED inspection procedures suggests that all concerned in the education of children who have SEN should follow recommendations to the letter. Approval of schools, via OFSTED and then by prospective parents, means a continued supply of pupils, thereby maintaining or increasing numbers of pupils on roll. Schools which adopt cooperative procedures may be more inclined to project a positive ethos to all concerned, ensuring that they communicate their effectiveness to as wide an audience as possible.

SECTION TWO

ADVOCACY AND SELF-ADVOCACY IN SCHOOLS: MAKING THINGS HAPPEN

Whatever constrains the development of advocacy in schools, our arguments in the preceding section have noted a range of benefits for children, teachers and the schools and classrooms in which they work. Persuading those who find advocacy either threatening or irrelevant to the child's 'real work' is a task which, we now suggest, is best tackled by offering a number of practical examples of pupil involvement in the organisation of learning and school management. The illustrations provided in the forthcoming section show the relevance of these approaches to teachers' practices; at the same time, however, they may suggest that, for many schools, there is some way to go before good practice is established.

First, Rena Harris-Cooksley and Robert Catt describe and discuss some ways in which primary school children have been involved in the maintenance of an orderly learning environment. They identify self-advocacy as the opportunity for children to engage in discussions amongst themselves and with their teachers in order to overcome difficulties in classroom management. In these discussions the importance of self-esteem in learning and the needs of both children and teachers are highlighted. Rena Harris-Cooksley describes what is essentially a behavioural approach, and in the final discussion, this way of working is critically examined by Robert Catt from the standpoint of a more humanistic approach. The ensuing dialogue reminds us that such enterprises must grow out of a holistic philosophy of teaching, rather than being grafted on as a mechanistic technique.

In the following chapter, a practising lecturer uses drama to show how one subject within the National Curriculum encompasses an empowering approach. Tom Sweeney begins by establishing two principles which, he argues, are fundamental to the process. These are the importance of non-verbal communication and the development of self-expression through empathy. The writer then sets out a range of social and cultural considerations which provide a context for his work. There follows a series of practical examples of drama activities which provide opportunities for all children to contribute in a positive way. Tom Sweeney has used his own expertise in drama to identify some valuable learning experiences. However, we would remind the reader that this is not the only subject which offers such scope; by careful examination of their current practices most teachers should be able to find similar opportunities in other subjects.

The third chapter in this section moves the reader from the classroom to the whole school. Jacquie Coulby and David Coulby describe the involvement of children in the management of a small primary school. This participation encompasses both policy and practice. Whilst the authors make no claim for the originality of the approaches they describe, the examples given by them are indicative of the possibilities that pupil involvement offers. So, the authors describe the development of the school's behaviour policy and the way in which the children's input has generated a highly positive school ethos. Such a philosophy is strengthened by an emphasis on equality: Jacquie Coulby and David Coulby provide accessible examples of good practice which are again drawn from this socially mixed primary school. Finally they examine the involvement of pupils and parents in the school curriculum, and conclude by illustrating the relevance of each of the strategies they describe to the empowerment of children who have special educational needs.

Sarah Sandow develops the theme of partnership by exploring the relationship between parents and the different levels of decision making in educational provision for children who have SEN. She focuses on the importance of good liaison between parents and teachers and provides illustrations of home-school communications which have both positive and negative impact. Whilst these affect all children, the author specifically reviews the current relationship between schools and parents of children who have SEN. She concludes by suggesting that the involvement of parents needs to be broadened beyond the needs of their own children if advocacy is to be fully effective.

The final chapter in this section looks at recent developments in the involvement of a wider circle of professionals in supporting advocacy. Irvine Gersch and Barbara Gersch write from their experience of working as part of a multi-disciplinary team. From the perspective of an educational psychologist and a local authority officer, they present a review of recent changes in practice as a precursor to a series of examples taken from some of their work in schools. The involvement of children as witnesses in legal proceedings has prompted professional consideration of their needs in the formal atmosphere of the court. The self-presentation skills which children should develop in school, perhaps as a result of the initiatives described in the whole of Section 2 of this book, are vital to their successful participation in such an adult environment. Finally the authors report a small survey of professional opinion about advocacy and self-advocacy and identify a number of matters relating to the relationship between children and those working on their behalf.

What may strike the reader is that all of these writers have been describing ways of working which are good practice in *any* school and with children with a wide range of differences, aptitudes and achievements. This is deliberate. An inclusive school, like an inclusive education system, should be offering these opportunities to *all* children. The curriculum, even the National Curriculum, is not a meaningful framework for education if it is not constructed in the service of empowerment.

Together, these chapters show that there is considerably more potential than constraint in the use of interventions which promote advocacy. The final section of this book will consider the actions which might be necessary if teachers and whole schools are to realise the potential of such ideas.

Chapter 2.1

CLASSROOM STRATEGIES FOR TEACHER AND PUPIL SUPPORT

Rena Harris-Cooksley and Robert Catt

In this chapter we adopt a case-study approach to the role adopted by a teacher-researcher who, as a member of a Behaviour Support Team, intervened to overcome the specific classroom management difficulties of an experienced but struggling teacher. The teacher-researcher acted as advocate for both the harassed classroom teacher herself and a group of pupils who had, seemingly, opted out of learning and who had become extremely disruptive. The support offered took the form of mediation between and the reconciliation of some conflicting purposes and oppositional approaches, together with the initiation of a series of classroom management strategies.

Much of our chapter will be descriptive, even anecdotal, and will draw upon:
- the teacher-researcher's field notes;
- discussion with the class-teacher involved;
- comments and illustrative drawings from pupils;
- evaluation and observation notes from a teaching
  colleague.

Of more than peripheral interest, too, is the collaborative approach which informs this chapter and, working within an essentially naturalistic paradigm, we aim to weave together a number of different voices to form a pattern illustrating the importance of self-esteem in learning and to emphasise the need for pupils as well as their teachers to be able to operate with some sense of dignity and self-worth. Ethical issues have been carefully weighed; the anonymity of all those involved, other than the teacher-researcher herself, has been ensured; we are particularly grateful to the classroom teacher who has participated in and encouraged this retrospective portrayal of the difficulties with which she was at that time confronted.

Our chapter ends with some reflective points drawn from a discussion between the two authors.

Figure 1: Before we started.

Classrooms, teachers, talking and learning

> If speech in childhood lays the foundation for a lifetime's thinking, then how can we prize a silent classroom? Britton (1987)

The role of languagein learning, and talk in particular, is an acknowledged and well-established feature of current practice. The rise of 'oracy' within the past thirty years has been thoroughly explored and documented (cf MaClure *et al.*, 1988) and once seemingly esoteric theories emphasising the relationship between language and the development of thought have been presented in accessible forms (cf Wood,1990). A welcome feature of recent classroom research is an examination of discourse detail drawing attention to the mechanisms, strategies and complexities which characterise classroom dialogue. On a more practical note and particularly useful for busy teachers are those organisational suggestions which are so coherently expressed in the NCC's Teaching, Talking and Learning Key series (NCC, 1991) built largely upon the very successful work of the National Oracy Project.

Our concern in this chapter, however, is that despite the acknowledged value of talk in classrooms, its management can be so problematic - and is particularly so in the case we shall be exploring.

Non -participant Field Notes (First Visit)

Teacher reluctant to go into class.
At desk - involved with nearest pupils.
Requested quiet for register.
Six pupils arrive late.
Some still noisy - moving around room ignoring request to sit down for quiet reading.
X refused to co-operate with instruction to move on to carpet. Teacher didn't argue - said o.k. Other pupils: 'That's not fair'...'He always gets what he wants'
Pupils on carpet - very restless: shoving, poking each other, continuing conversations.
Teacher interacting with nearest pupils.
No positive feedback to pupils.
Pupils return to places very noisy, pushing: 'He's got my...Can't find my...'.

Pupils not organised for task. Calling out: 'This is boring...You're copying me....Miss!'
Six pupils very loud, calling out, two sulking, out of seats.
Some refusing to work: 'I'm not doing this. This is rubbish'.
M shouting. Teacher tells him to work on carpet.
Teacher interacting with two pupils. No feedback to class.
Girls mainly on task - no contact with teacher.
Many pupils off-task but not re-directed.
Playtime - pupils leave room without tidying up: rush out.
Chairs, bags everywhere.

Context

The ten-week programme of support took place in a co-educational mainstream middle-school in an outer London Borough. The school had a mixed catchment area and strong links with parents.

The Year 6 mixed-ability group comprised 17 boys and 9 girls from a variety of social and ethnic backgrounds. Although the gender imbalance was acknowledged the school's senior managers felt it was not possible to organise the class in any other way. The class teacher, however, felt that the gender imbalance contributed to the difficulties which pupils experienced in their interpersonal relationships within the classroom.

There were further concerns about the special needs of several children within the class. Two pupils had statements of special educational need and both pupils had difficulties in establishing and maintaining friendships amongst the peer group. The class teacher felt this was largely the result of the effects that their often angry aggressive outbursts had on the flow of lessons. Their behaviour often interrupted lessons when the class teacher's attention was taken up with refereeing disagreements or disciplining inappropriate behaviour such as calling out, name calling and refusal to co-operate with instructions. The other pupils in the group seemed unable to cope with this behaviour and were reluctant to work in groups which included either of the statemented pupils. The class teacher reported that many of her planned lessons were either abandoned or that learning outcomes were unsatisfactory from her point of view. She neither felt that the classroom environment was one which was 'calm and purposeful' (DES, 1989) nor that the pupils had the social skills which would enable them to build relationships and handle the unreasonable behaviour of others.

Concern amongst parents, other staff, pupils and the class teacher herself was such that an urgent request for help was made to the Borough's Behavioural Support Team.

The class teacher was experienced in working across the middle-school age-range and felt confident in her ability as a teacher. She described her role as that of 'a facilitator for learning' and had always structured her classes in order to foster 'a child-centred and collaborative' approach heavily dependent upon group work. Although she used a teaching style which she had always found to be successful, she reported almost immediately that there were difficulties in managing the class. During the first half of the Autumn term there were increasing difficulties initially attributed to individual pupils but then ascribed to the class as a whole. She began to feel that she was failing and, uncharacteristically, began to lose confidence in her abilities. She sought the help and advice of her headteacher and it was at this point - within the first half-term - that the school made a request for help.

'Now the bell's gone!'
Extracts from Working Notes Following an Initial Interview with the Class Teacher

The class teacher spoke about specific behavioural difficulties saying that the worst things seemed to be: '...calling out...name calling...never listening to each other or me...fighting in the classroom....spending more time sorting out their arguments than working...have to abandon most 'fun' activities like practical group task or PE games...they can't or won't follow instructions...very noisy all the time...I end up shouting at them then they get moody...Now the bell's gone and I'll have to go back in there...It's only Monday morning...There's the whole week to get through yet!

Strategies
'They just don't listen!'

It is particularly important when setting up a teacher-outsider partnership to discuss problems, their probable causes and possible solutions (Bowers, 1989)

Figure 2: '...never listening to each other or me...'

Following initial observation of the class at work a discussion immediately took place in an informal and non-threatening setting, between the headteacher, class teacher and the teacher-researcher. A variety of strategies, including work with individual pupils, was considered before an 'advocate' approach was agreed whereby the teacher-researcher would work collaboratively for and with the class teacher and the class as a whole. A shared understanding of the problem was established, together with desired outcomes against which teaching roles could be negotiated and a programme of support could be planned.

Information and observations were pooled allowing the class teacher and teacher-researcher to establish broad aims:

- to encourage pupils to develop skills and knowledge which would help them build and sustain positive relationships thereby enabling them to work co-operatively in groups;

- to use a collaborative teaching approach which would support the class teacher in acquiring and taking ownership of some techniques for effective classroom management so that she could encourage the generalisation and maintenance of skills taught to pupils;

and immediate goals:

- that pupils should respond positively towards one another and towards adults;
- that pupils should be able to use the skills taught to achieve a group task.

The programme was planned to cover a ten-week period with the teacher-researcher team-teaching with the class teacher during two regular mornings each week in either the classroom or main hall as appropriate. Protected timetable time was also set aside for half an hour during each Monday morning for planning and reflection.

Pressure from the class teacher influenced the decision to begin the programme of support immediately. It was also immediately clear that it would be necessary to agree a set of well-defined boundaries for behaviour within the classroom setting. Although the programme was planned using a structured approach suggested by Spence (1980) flexibility was retained so that the sessions could be tailored to meet the emerging needs of the group. This is a factor identified by Curtis (1983) as important for the success of a social skills training with primary school pupils. A three-point plan was agreed whereby pupils could be encouraged to generalise and maintain the skills they had learned:

i) skills taught should be related to the settings in which the behaviour was expected to occur - e.g. listening to each other and the class teacher especially in the classroom environment - but should also be reinforced in other settings - e.g. the main hall;

ii) collaboration between the class teacher and the teacher-researcher would enable the identification and reinforcement of target behaviours on a daily basis;

iii) all pupils should be given opportunities to work in groups which included positive role models so that peer pressure could be effectively harnessed.

Pupil Perceptions - Selected Extracts from the Teacher-Researcher's Field Notes
'Your mother lives in a wheelie bin!'

Before starting on the programme I knew it would be necessary to establish a relationship with the class. I visited the school with the intention of introducing myself to the group. I was very nervous. I'd never met a class quite like this. They took no notice of me whatsoever. I think, quite genuinely, they had no interest in yet another adult who'd just walked into their classroom. After a while I said, quietly, 'Raise your hand if you can hear me.' Slowly - thankfully - some did, then others noticed and yelled 'Shutup!' The noise level dropped until there was quiet and their attention was focused on me.

I grabbed this first opportunity to acknowledge those who had responded immediately. I said how pleased I was that everyone was now quiet and how I had been particularly impressed with the way in which some members of the class had been ready very quickly: they were sitting up, looking towards me, having stopped their conversations.

My agenda at this point was to set out some ground rules and establish expectations - mine of them and, perhaps more importantly, to find out what they expected from me! What had I let myself in for, I wondered?

I introduced myself to the class telling them some of the kinds of activities we would be doing. I began by telling them something about my job and how I worked and was quickly told 'We know why you're here. It's because we're naughty!' As I got to know them better they said things like: 'Teachers don't like us. Nobody wants to teach us.' I asked them what they felt 'the problem' was and they quickly identified some familiar difficulties. They said there was far too much noise. People were always shouting out and calling across the room. There was a lot of name calling. Some told me how upsetting the name calling could be, particularly when it was aimed at their mothers. A favourite taunt was 'Your mother lives in a wheelie-bin!' and this would usually be enough to start a fight. They claimed that school was boring; that the teacher was always shouting at them because some people in the class were always getting out of their seats, walking round the class and banging rulers on the desk. During this initial discussion I took every opportunity to reinforce and clarify the behaviour I wanted to see happening. For example, I ignored shouted out answers/contributions, turning to someone with their hand up saying 'I'm going to ask you because you have your hand up' or 'good, you waited for your turn to speak.'

Three Rules

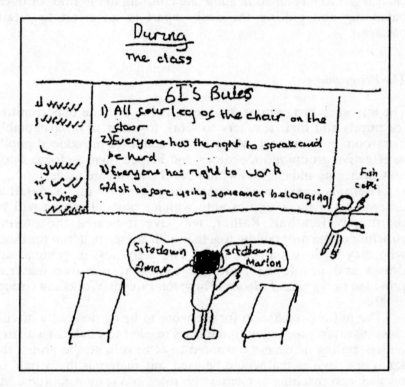

Figure 3: Owning the rules

I used a good many prompts to establish three ground rules which I wrote up on the board. In a way I was trying to establish with the class the basic conditions they would need if teachers were not to shout at them and if they were going to do interesting work. It was heavy going but I used a lot of questions: 'Why do teachers get angry with you?' and 'What makes it difficult to be heard by other people?' and I re-worked the answers, 'So it's better if only one person speaks at a time' etc. (ignoring the shouters) so that they had some sense of owning the rules:

i) everyone has the right to speak and be heard;

ii) everyone has the right to opt out of an activity (but they would be
helped to do it at the end of the session so no cop outs!);
iii) all four legs of the chair should remain on the floor all the time.

(This was an essential ground rule because swinging around on the
chair legs often resulted in someone crashing to the floor or over-
balancing and pulling the desks apart in an effort to retain
balance.)

The Programme

The ten-week programme was designed to provide opportunities
for pupils and their teachers to work together in an acceptable
classroom environment. Many of the activities introduced pupils
to effective grouping procedures and helped them to focus upon
how decisions and choices within the classroom are made.

There is insufficient space here to provide a detailed
description of the activities with which many colleagues will be
thoroughly familiar. Rather, we have indicated the outline
structure of the programme together with source material for those
who may wish to pursue ideas. The activities, in general, are
drawn and developed from the excellent resource material
provided in *Ways and Means* (Kingston Friends Workshop Group,
1989).

The initial preparation for the work to be carried out with this
class involved meeting with the class teacher to establish a shared
understanding of what we wanted to achieve with the group, the
kinds of activities that would be used, any materials that would be
needed, and reaching agreement on roles and responsibilities. My
agreed role was to plan the programme, prepare any materials that
would be necessary, lead the sessions and to take responsibility for
classroom management during the sessions.

The first session was used to establish the ground rules which
would be in place and to make clear to the pupils my expectations
as far as behaviour and participation were concerned. As this class
had been formed from two other classes and I had not taught them
before, I felt it was important that they should begin by getting to
know each other and by establishing rules which would allow
everyone to feel comfortable within the group.

Once the rules had been established, the class teacher agreed
to use some time during the week to allow the pupils to record
them and make a poster which could then be put up at the front of
the room. In this way anyone who came into the room would be

able to see what the rules were during the sessions. It also meant that the rules could be referred to and reinforced when necessary.

This process of establishing ground rules was in itself an opportunity for me to begin to highlight any positive points that emerged. For example, I was able to draw attention to 'good' behaviour that was already happening - examples of attentive listening, turn-taking and following instructions. I was able to give the pupils some feedback about what they were able to do. This was important for both them and their teacher as both parties had been focusing on what was not happening, e.g. '*They* never listen; *they* can't get on' - '*She's* always shouting; *she* doesn't listen to us; teachers don't like us because we're naughty and noisy...'.

The next step was to use this feedback as a way of beginning to look at how positive qualities can be represented as symbols. They came up with various suggestions such as an ear to represent attentive listening, a smiley face or joined hands to represent friendship. I led the discussion so that it began to focus on pupils themselves and things they were good at or enjoyed doing. The aim at this point was to provide an opportunity for them to exchange information about each other in a safe way, i.e. they would be able to disclose information without feeling awkward or being embarrassed by the negative comments of others.

Week One

I used affirmation activities from *Ways and Means* (Kingston Friends, *op.cit*, p.34) as introductory 'warm ups'. These provided opportunities for the pupils not only to get to know one another, but to focus on themselves too. We began by making name badges. This was an activity which combined Labels and Likes with Labels and Goods. The task was to design a name badge which gives three positive messages about the wearer:

i) something I like to do (e.g. read; listen to music; play sport)
ii) something I am good at (e.g. football, computer games, swimming);
iii) something good about me (e.g. friendly, helpful, sharing).

The badges were made on circles of card and were worn for every session.

Week Two

The badges were central to a follow-up activity: Interviews and Introductions. This encouraged the pupils to speak and listen to one another and then, taking turns, they shared one piece of information about each other with the whole class. The discussion which followed the activity highlighted the point that it is much easier to talk about someone else's positive attributes than one's own. We were then able to look at the difference between being able to acknowledge one's strengths and boasting and the feelings involved in this self-disclosure. Many of the pupils said that they would have felt embarrassed to speak to the group about themselves and were worried that people would make fun of them. Others expressed surprise about some of the things they found out about each other.

Week Three

I wanted the pupils to begin to see each other in a more positive light and to begin to explore the feelings they experienced when receiving positive feedback. I began to introduce further affirmation and listening activities drawn, again, from *Ways and Means* (Kingston Friends, *op.cit.* pp. 39, 42, 47, 48).

'Lifemaps', an activity from *Global Teacher, Global Learner* (Pike and Selby, 1990, pp. 109, 110) was used to provide further opportunities for information sharing and finding out what sorts of life experiences they had in common. Some of these experiences included the death of a pet or a grandparent, separation from parents because of hospitalisation, significant changes in pupils' lives such as moving school or class, moving house or friends moving away.

Again, my aim was to enable the pupils to practise speaking and listening to one another, and to support them in valuing one another by modelling empathetic responses.

Reflection at the end of each session was an important part of the work. We looked at a number of aspects of the sessions - these included looking at the feelings experienced by individuals during the activities and then attempting to relate these to other life experiences. So, for example, when individuals spoke of their feelings of frustration or anger when not being listened to, they were encouraged to try and imagine what other people feel like in the same situation (parents, teachers, peers). In this way, it was possible to draw out general principles and to relate these to interpersonal relationships.

At the end of each session the pupils were also asked to reflect upon their behaviour and to assess how well they thought they had managed as individuals on a scale of 1 - 5. In later sessions when they had been involved in group tasks, they were asked to assess how well they had managed both as individuals and as a group. They were encouraged to consider how they had contributed to the achievement of the group task. I was hoping that in this way they would begin to see how as individuals they had a responsibility to the group and to be able to identify behaviour which was both helpful and unhelpful.

Week Four

To reinforce these principles we used the hall for what we called grouping activities. These started as very simple games which were intended to provide opportunities for the pupils to be in groups with others for very short periods of time.

Getting into groups was a major area of conflict with the pupils in this class. They usually refused to co-operate unless they were in friendship groups. In view of this I was anxious to present the grouping activities in as non-threatening a way as possible.

The first session here involved the pupils in simply walking around the hall on their own, not having any contact with one another and following any instructions given by me:
 i) walk around the hall slowly;
 ii) when I call 'Stop', touch the floor and change direction.
After three or four circuits I changed the instructions slightly:
 i) walk around the hall on your own;
 ii) when I call out a number (e.g. 'Three') make a group of that size with the nearest people to you;
 iii) as soon as you are in a group sit down on the floor.

Positive feedback was given to reinforce success - e.g., 'Good...Well done....This group was ready first: they got together quickly and sat down.'

The next step was to form mixed gender groups which I knew would not be easy. Again it was necessary to make this 'safe' so, using the same numbers activity, I changed the instructions slightly by breaking down the number called out, e.g. 'Five: that's a three and a two' which meant three boys and two girls, or vice versa. Again, groups were asked to sit on the floor as soon as they were formed. Praise and positive feedback were used to reinforce success.

Inevitably some groups had difficulty in forming quickly but, rather than focusing on individuals, subsequent discussion was directed towards the procedures that had been helpful in enabling groups to get together easily and fluently.

As they became more relaxed about getting into groups in this setting, I began to introduce simple tasks so that instructions became more demanding:

i)   when I call out a number get into a group of that size;
ii) sit down when you as a group are ready;
iii) now make a shape of, e.g. letter A; a number 4, a house etc.

These activities were great fun and the pupils enjoyed their sessions very much. The discussion at the end of each session looked at how the groups had functioned, how tasks had been achieved, at individual contributions and participation and decision-making processes. In some groups leaders and organisers emerged whilst in other groups this was not so apparent. Where one group was consistently less successful we looked together at what might be going wrong for them. To help in this process we reflected on what had contributed to achievement in the successful groups. Sometimes I reorganised the groups to enable some pupils to work with others who were good role models so that they could have the experience of working with a successful group.

Another strategy I used to help groups was to allow those who were successful to be observed carrying out a task, then using discussion to identify the things that helped the group work together.

When discussing ideas about what people did that was helpful in enabling the group to achieve the task, pupils were able to identify certain behaviours as important:

- sharing ideas;
- listening to each other;
- everyone having something to do which they felt they were able to do;
- being able to stay cheerful even if you don't get your own way;
- helping each other.

Week Five

The classroom sessions used activities which focused on the component skills for successful group work. *Global Teacher; Global Learner* (Pike and Selby, *op. cit.* , Chapters 7 and 8) and *Ways and Means* (Kingston Friends, *op. cit.*, pp. 49-59) provided a more substantial basis for the development of listening skills, enabling us to establish a set of classroom rules through negotiation. These activities involved going through the process of reaching agreement and exploring feelings experienced along the way.

This was an important part of the whole programme as we were dealing with the very issues these pupils found the most difficult to embrace. The 'Steps to Solutions' activity (Kingston Friends, *op. cit.*, p. 103) provided a most useful framework for looking at areas of real disagreement. It helped the pupils and their teacher to distance themselves from the problem and see it as *a problem* rather than *their problem* or *my problem*. It was a technique which both pupils and teacher continued to use even after the end of the programme.

Week Six

We then moved on to establish a set of classroom rules using the principles of the negotiation activities, 'Picture Ranking' and 'Agreeing to Disagree' (Kingston Friends, *op.cit.*, p. 95). A list of possible classroom rules was generated by both pupils and adults. The rules were then written on separate cards and displayed around the room. The next step was to agree a set of between three and five positively framed rules. I felt it was important that the pupils were clear about how they should behave rather than how they should not behave. This would provide an effective scaffold for both them and their teacher in that they would know when they were behaving appropriately and, by implication, when they were not. The teacher would be able to reinforce this by offering feedback and praise appropriately. This involved going through the process of reaching agreement and exploring the feelings experienced along the way.

At this point in the programme parents were involved when we asked them to support the system of rules, rewards and sanctions put together and agreed by the pupils. It was important to have parental support as it reinforced the feeling of ownership for the pupils and gave status to the work they had been involved in. It was also a means of sharing the work with parents.

Week Seven

The focus was now on group tasks with opportunities to practise skills in 'real' settings. This was important as it enabled pupils to have experience of how these skills could help them in two important ways:

- they would be able to form positive relationships with one another;
- they would be able to work together more effectively and therefore increase their opportunities to learn.

We used the co-operative squares activity (Kingston Friends, *op. cit.*, p.63 and Pike and Selby, *op. cit.*, p. 166) as a means of raising awareness of the issues or demands of group co-operation and to look at the feelings associated with group task achievement.

An activity used at this stage was a non-verbal task which we called tower building: the numbers grouping strategy was used from Week 2 to arrange pupils in groups of four. Each group was given six sheets of paper and six strips of sellotape. The task was to see which group could build the highest, most attractive, most stable tower. 'Cheating', i.e. talking, resulted in the group forfeiting one sheet of paper. The activity was then repeated using discussion as a means of communication.

Weeks Eight and Nine

These two weeks were used for a group task: 'Desert Island Classroom' (Kingston Friends, *op. cit.*, p. 117). This was a means of practising all the skills and techniques we had been working to develop and relating them to curriculum-based activities. Pupils were encouraged to take responsibility for both individual and group achievement. They were required to discuss, plan and negotiate, report back and listen in both small and large group settings. It was necessary to agree rules, follow instructions and reflect on individual and group performance. In order for them to achieve this they had to use sequences of behaviour involving problem-solving, perspective-taking and self-evaluation. These are the complex process skills which Curtis (1983) and Davies (1983) attribute to social competence. The level of adult help required by the class for this activity was minimal. Observation notes from these sessions confirm that there was a high level of co-operation between group members during these activities.

Figure 4: Active listening

Week Ten

The final session was used for an evaluation of the whole programme. This was an opportunity for pupils and teachers to reflect upon what had been achieved and to look at 'what next'.

Did the programme succeed?
No inflated claims for the success of the programme are being made. However, observable change in classroom behaviour and evidence of the improved esteem of both the class teacher and

pupils at the end of the ten-week period can be drawn from these sources:

Independent Observation

The observations of an advisory teacher were invited and, as these selected notes indicate, there was some clear contrast with observations made at the beginning of the programme:

- Session: Finishing off work - variety of tasks: Maths, Science and Language work.
- Pupils working in pairs or threes.
- Noise level low - talking quietly; mainly girl-girl, boy-boy interactions.
- Request for help - boys to adjacent girl who gave help then returned to her task.
- X refused to work initially; teacher-pupil negotiation successful - on-task now.
- Two pupils doing science experiment - negotiated roles - who does what, what to do first discussed then started.
- Teacher moving around room from group to group.
- Sudden loud outburst - M shouting. Teacher ignores at first then gives 'look' - quiet now.
- Most pupils seem on-task - writing, drawing, reading.
- M calling out. Teacher gives verbal request not to do it again.
- Feedback to pupils is positive - 'That's good!'. Yes', etc.

Staff Feedback

A number of the class teacher's colleagues were interested in the programme and its activities; they were a source of encouragement and positive commentary upon the improved progress of the class.

Reflections from the Class Teacher

Comments upon the programme from the class teacher indicate both that change is possible but that progress is neither smooth nor unproblematic -

I'm much more relaxed. I accept things I wouldn't have done before - for example, if 90% of the class is working, I'm happy.

The class is now beginning to gel. They were very rude to one another, took no responsibility for their actions, did no work unless it was formal. They could do no group work at all even when choosing their own groups.

The class is now beginning to behave - but some days it's like going back to square one! They work well in groups that they chose: book making, model making present no problems now. They still have real problems listening to instructions - if we could remedy this. They still fight amongst each other and this must be improved if possible.

I begin to feel it possible to make the class one real unit - that they can feel a sense of belonging; that they can work independently and take responsibility for their own actions so that they can take pride in their work and their classroom.

Pupil Evaluation

Throughout the programme and usually at the end of each Monday session, pupils were encouraged to reflect upon their behaviour and progress. Towards the end of the programme a more direct evaluation was conducted and, in addition to some detailed discussion, pupils were asked to draw themselves as they were behaving before the programme began and as they were behaving currently. Some of these drawings have been included here and, although the crudity of the evaluation tool is acknowledged there is, surely, some evidence of pride in the progress made and of increased esteem. Here, however, we would be cautious in that some drawings and pupil comments indicated a certain amount of realistic doubt that gains made might not last beyond the support programme.

However, as we indicated in our introduction, our purpose here is not to recommend a specific and unproblematic package of strategies. Rather, we have tried to describe something of what can be achieved through carefully-planned intervention and advocacy: working, that is, on behalf of others to achieve orderly and dignified conditions within which learning can best take place. Different classroom environments and different contexts will require different approaches and, rather than working towards a seemingly neat closure, we feel it more in keeping with the dialogical construction of our chapter to conclude with some selected reflections drawn from a discussion between the two authors.

Discussion

RC: What I take from your programme of - let's call it intervention and support - is that optimistic belief that things can be changed. So many of us have probably been in that 'The bell's gone!' situation but what's needed is that belief that this isn't inevitable. Things can be done. Change is possible.

RHC: My experience is that classroom factors like those I met at the beginning of the programme just result in negative outcomes for everybody. Self-esteem falls; feelings of helplessness and hopelessness are expressed. Pupils and teacher respond angrily or apathetically towards one another. They all come to view themselves as non-achievers and label themselves as people who can't manage. Labels are then applied by other staff, pupils and parents. The class becomes the difficult class. The teacher is seen as ineffective. The negative cycle perpetuates itself and the learning environment deteriorates. And that can't go on. The role of the teacher in my view, is to find a way of allowing herself and her pupils to speak and be heard in an environment where mutual respect is encouraged, acknowledged and practised.

RC: Do you mean giving dignity to each other?

RHC: Yes, dignity and status. Giving status by identifying good role models and amplifying success. And this can be acquired without shouting loudly. It can be done - but teachers know this - with a look, a comment, a nod or a smile. By showing approval and giving feedback and reassurance.

RC: And I've noticed in all our discussions that you never point the finger at anyone. You never say it's the pupils' fault or it's bad teaching or bad organisation.

RHC: That's right. I wasn't there to make value judgements, but then it was easier for me - I was detached, I didn't get worn down by it. But I could sympathise wholeheartedly with the class teacher's situation. I'd been there myself. With this particular group it was hard work. I had to use all my own tried and tested strategies to keep them with me for an hour. It was easy to see how she could be worn down by the end of the day.

RC: Isn't there a danger, though, of ignoring the bigger picture? I mean the class teacher clearly felt there were organisational problems - the gender split within the group, for example - and shouldn't they be tackled at a management level rather than putting the emphasis on what might be called coping strategies?

RHC: I'm not saying that poor organisation shouldn't be criticised or should be ignored. But in this case that was the situation and, although senior management were aware of the difficulties, the class teacher just had to get on with it. Like most teachers she was working in a situation which was far from ideal and she had to cope. But I wasn't just helping her to cope and that's the advocacy thing. My role was to be an advocate for the teacher and the pupils. I was trying to be advocate for them and their advocate for her. That meant mediating between them and engaging them all in activities where they could see things from another's perspective - like setting the classroom rules and taking turns in speaking, for example. Both parties were able to exchange views, reach agreement and disclose how it felt not to be listened to; to have to give up something you wanted.

RC: A good deal has been written about classroom environments. - that need for a kind of psychological safety which is so important but which was clearly lacking in this case.

RHC: We certainly gave a lot of attention to the physical layout of the classroom and the way in which pupils were grouped. In addition the class teacher was introduced to a number of techniques and strategies. There's nothing particularly original about them: they're ideas I've developed from various sources, as we all do. But these weren't just about coping; they were about constructing a worthwhile learning environment. Underpinning everything we did was the attention and feedback given to listening and following instructions and lots of opportunities to practise were provided. When we were team-teaching I was always consciously trying to highlight the opportunities which presented themselves for acknowledging and praising appropriate pupil responses.

RC: You often talk about 'appropriate response' and 'behaviour' and 'reinforcement' and a lot of what you describe seems to derive from behaviourist psychology. As you know I feel uneasy about that because I think there's a tendency to overlook the deeper structures of teaching and learning and those processes which are less obviously observable. But then when I look over your programme in detail I don't think you're being merely 'behaviourist' in your approach: I think that you and the class teacher - like all good teachers - are quite rightly eclectic; you're drawing upon a range of useful theory. A crucial feature which, I think, takes the whole thing a stage further beyond the mere management of behaviour is your attention to reflection. This is particularly evident when you ask the pupils to give attention to what they've been doing in each session. I think you're getting close to what is called 'metacognition' - the idea of the mind turning back on itself. You did that repeatedly with the children and with the class teacher too when you went through that regular process of joint deliberation which involved far more than just planning things together.

RHC: Yes, I tried to do that but it needs a very explicit framework - a scaffold is the buzz word. The class teacher and I were able to agree about a framework in our weekly meetings and evaluation sessions. Then, when I was teaching the class, I'd ask pupils to reflect upon their achievements as individuals. I might do that through discussion by getting them to do it more formally on a one (could be better) to five (brilliant) scale. Then as we went on they were able to progress from self to group assessment so they were thinking about achievement on two levels - as individuals and as a group as a whole resulting from individual contributions to the group task. We talked about this a lot together - the pupils, the class teacher and I - at the end of every session where we'd always have a discussion. We looked at what we'd managed to do, what we felt we'd gained, if anything, and the needs emerging from the session. It was also a real social session in which to practise skills like listening to points of view, responding with relevant comments, valuing the comments of others and waiting for a turn to speak. And it helped us to generalise, to look at real problems in other social settings - things like friendship issues came up a lot for discussion. And what emerged strongly from that was what you might call the 'modelling' of appropriate ways of expressing feelings or making criticisms in a non-threatening way.

RC: We're back to dignity again.

RHC: Yes, it's all to do with self-perception, self-esteem and feeling that it's 'okay' to expect to be heard and to expect to be part of shaping what happens to you and around you in a classroom or school setting. That's what I mean when I talk about self-advocacy. Young people do have these social skills but sometimes they need to learn to use them appropriately if they're to conduct themselves with dignity. Our role as adults is to provide opportunities for and to enhance and accelerate developing skills like those we concentrated on here so that they can cope with the demands of the school and classroom setting and increase their learning opportunities.

RC: But don't we already know that?

RHC: Theoretically, yes. However, it seems to me that many adults seem to pay lip-service to the idea but don't follow it up in practical terms. You see, I'm talking about appropriate behaviour in classrooms which, for some teachers, might mean submissive behaviour. We're getting here into the debate on individual values and expectations.

RC: This is where your programme connects with my interest in speaking and listening. I absolutely agree that we need to structure opportunities to develop speaking and listening skills, and that means establishing orderly conditions. But that has to be done in the interests of genuine learning not just for ritual knowledge and control. I think that takes great skill, particularly in developing a purposeful dialogue with pupils, and it's something we don't always give enough attention to. But then when you're talking about advocacy it sometimes seems to me that you're talking about collaboration, about exchanging ideas. And that collaborative environment in education is certainly desirable but it's not something many colleagues enjoy. To them especially, your supportive programme might seem a bit of a luxury.

RHC: Well, it wasn't that because it was a pretty desperate situation. But I still feel that teachers can become advocates for each other through discussing their practice and problems and by adopting strategies of self-advocacy. But the trouble is, teachers don't get enough positive feedback themselves. Nobody tells them they're doing well and they need more of that.

RC: And more attention to research of this kind.

Chapter 2.2

CURRICULUM MATTERS: USING DRAMA TO EXTEND THE INVOLVEMENT OF CHILDREN WITH SPECIAL EDUCATIONAL NEEDS

Tom Sweeney

RENU : What did you actually do after you'd been to Pizza Hut?
PAUL : We went back to Dilip's house...
RENU : (interrupting) What did you do there?
PAUL : Well, we played a game, baseball, and painting...
RENU : (interrupting) And who won baseball?
PAUL : (smiling) I did.
RENU : Right.
MARY : (interjecting) Did you eat anything there?
PAUL :(thinks) ...
RENU : (continuing) OK, what did you do after the painting?
PAUL : Went home.
RENU : How did you go home?
PAUL : By bus.
RENU : What bus?
PAUL : 290.
MARY : }(together) What time was it..
RENU : }(together) Did you go home or did Dilip go with you?
PAUL : No...Danny...
MARY : }(together) What time was it when you got back to your house?
RENU : }(together) Right, where was...did you sit upstairs or downstairs?
PAUL : (nervous) We sat downstairs.
MARY : What time was it when you got back to your house?
PAUL : Ten minutes past nine... something like that.
MARY : Did you pass the school on your way back?
PAUL : (hesitates) Yeah.
MARY : Did you see anything there?
PAUL : No...(shakes head) no... I saw a lock broken there.
MARY : Did you see anyone walking around it?

PAUL : No.
RENU : And what time did you pass the school?
PAUL : Nine.

Introduction

The pupils in the extract are in role, they are normally two mild-mannered girls who prefer to allow others to lead discussion sessions. Here, they have been given the opportunity to interrogate a boy: he claims to have an alibi. They have prepared a number of questions and he finds himself under unexpected pressure in that his own previously prepared story is beginning to show signs of collapse. His two collaborators will soon find themselves in a similarly uncomfortable position. These boys are also in role: they are suspected of vandalism and the girls, in role as detectives, are trying to verify the plausibility of their alibis. Drama is being used to enable these Year 6 pupils to develop their inquiry skills and powers of communication.

The context of the classroom has been changed to facilitate this learning. Drama activities, and the fictional or pretend mode that is associated with this style of learning, is not only a means of enlivening the classroom but also a powerful medium for presenting pupils with real-ife challenges and opportunities. The teacher, in planning these activities, has paid close attention to a number of considerations that affect the context for speaking and listening. The normal context of classroom, teacher and pupils is suspended and altered to provide participants with an environment and opportunities to find their voices in different ways. Peter (1994. p. 2) acknowledges the contribution of drama to the development of language and lists a number of key points which have relevance to pupils with SEN. Included in this list are: symbolic understanding, vocabulary, articulation, accuracy, conversational competence, oracy and literacy.

The teacher can intervene to construct differing contexts by using drama to attend to some or all of the following factors that affect the spoken word. A number of these factors are suggested in the work of the Wiltshire Oracy Project (1989, p.9):

> The reason for talk; why it is taking place, what outcome is intended.

> The communicative purpose of the task or activity; what type(s) of talk will be necessary to complete the interaction satisfactorily, perhaps the task requires explanation, narration, questioning, negotiation or a combination of these and other types of talk?

The role expected of the speaker (real or imaginary); this could be an expert, an interviewee, a conspirator, a stranger?

The speaker's understanding of the topic is also important; will the speaker be confident of the material, to what extent is the speaker an expert either real or imaginary?

The location will affect the quality of the speaking and listening; drama is a medium for creating imaginary locations which create different demands to those normally found in the classroom, pupils may at times be expected to remain as themselves but in different circumstances or circumstances not yet encountered.

The audience can also be changed and varied through the use of drama; feedback given, or not given, by different audiences will affect the speaking and listening processes, individuals or groups may act in a friendly, supportive fashion but may also be briefed on other occasions to be challenging, inquisitive, perhaps even aggressive.

The speaker's perception of the situation will therefore vary and this can be facilitated by the teacher; confidence, stress, urgency can be in some measure set up by the teacher's manipulation of the factors affecting the interaction.

In addition, the support provided by the teacher to pupils in terms of advice, guidance, equipment, notes, props if appropriate is also a factor to be considered when establishing the context for talk.

It is the intention of this chapter to indicate how dramatic role can be a powerful and effective medium to influence these factors so that the context of the classroom is adapted and changed to explore a variety of language demands in order to give young people a 'voice' so they can become effective communicators.

It is clear that when children are fully engaged in drama, emotionally, physically and intellectually, the language they use to express ideas reveals that their emotional engagement stimulates intellectual growth. The intimate relationship between intellect and emotion is clearly seen in the expressive language identified... the incidence of which was far greater than that found in other classroom contexts (Parsons *et al* ..1984, p.21).

The fictional context not only enables pupils to experience a range of language uses and a sense of audience, but as evidenced in the extract above, there is the opportunity to bring together thought and feeling; the emotional commitment given to the roles enables pupils to develop an understanding of the power of language.

It is commonplace for such activities to be seen as marginal for children with special educational needs. However, the truth is that they are even more necessary for children who have a constant experience of failure and even ridicule from their peers. It is possible to 'practise' the skills of self-expression and self-assertion, and often impossible to develop those skills without practice. Furthermore, theatrical approaches to the use of drama in the curriculum tend to concentrate on those children who are already confident and articulate speakers whilst relegating the others to the chorus or non-speaking parts.

In proposing a case for 'one drama for all', whereby pupils with special educational needs are entitled to fundamentally similar drama processes as 'mainstream' children, Peter makes reference to post-Warnock practices of integration and mixed-ability teaching:

> The teacher of drama, now more than ever, needs to be able to differentiate his/her teaching to work with pupils of any ability, whether in a mainstream or special school situation. It needs to be stated here, that in any case, pupils of similar chronological age may be at the same level of emotional maturity, whether or not they are deemed to have 'special educational needs' (Peter, 1994, p.4).

This then is the background to a chapter that is essentially practical and designed to give brief accounts of tasks, activities and ideas that have worked with pupils sharing a wide range of abilities and maturities.

Two principles

Paradoxically, the suggested activities which are to follow in this chapter rest on two principles that might at first sight appear to undermine notions of advocacy and self-advocacy. Firstly, initial work is based on non-verbal forms of communication so that pupils begin to find their 'voice' through more physical activities rather than an expectation to present ideas verbally at the outset. Secondly, the ideas largely centre on the notion of pretence or fictional 'as if' circumstances so that pupils develop powers of self- expression by giving voice to the thoughts, feelings and experiences of others. In pretending to speak as another person, or as oneself in other circumstances, individuals can explore and experiment with approaches to self-expression and self-assertion. The activities and tasks designed on these principles are intended to unblock the obstacles that prevent many children expressing themselves and interacting with others.

These activities will also provide opportunities for the learning necessary to accomplish the transactions of everyday life and an understanding of their own thought processes. Perhaps we need to remind ourselves that for many young people having a voice will not mean giving formal speeches or developing the skills of an orator but will require   social interaction and effective communication in the work place and in the community.

> Although no committee would ever have composed Beethoven's 5th symphony, it is unlikely that any individual could have sent a rocket to the moon. A great deal of human achievement will in future be the result of teamwork (Wragg, 1984).

Opportunities to practise presentational skills, both in formal and informal settings, are important, but the processes associated with collaborative group work are also a key feature of the activities suggested in this chapter. The social learning associated with drama should not be underestimated in this respect.

The roots of this work are grounded in both theatrical practice and educational research. The literacy projects inspired by the Brazilian educationalist Freire, have in turn influenced the theatrical ideas of Boal whose work acknowledges the power of theatre and its potential to give a voice to the oppressed (Boal, 1979). His ideas in relation to what is termed 'image' theatre and 'forum' theatre make a crucial link between feelings and intellect, between visual and verbal modes of expression, in using dramatic conventions to provide possibilities for involvement and active participation in the processes that shape our lives :

> the spectator delegates no power to the character (or actor) either to act or to think in his place; on the contrary, he himself assumes the protagonic role, changes the dramatic action, tries out solutions, discusses plans for change - in short, trains himself for real action (Boal, 1979 p.122).

There is also a substantial body of literature, including National Curriculum documents, that supports the need for drama in the development of speaking and listening skills. Drama enables pupils to become involved in the immediacy of events as 'lived through' experience rather than action that is merely reported. This concrete experience enables pupils to engage with topics, materials and people at a level that is both appropriate in terms of effective learning and safe in terms of its psychological distance.

A framework of drama activities provides conditions that are consistent with the ingredients for successful language learning, i.e. opportunities for real interactions, opportunities to use the imagination and an environment that provides for a range of language experiences.

It is unfortunate that it is these activities which are curtailed for children with SEN, because they need to be withdrawn for extra work with the 'basics'. The diminution of emphasis in the National Curriculum on 'speaking and listening' makes this more likely. Neelands (1992) suggests a 'mother tongue' model of learning, which has proved successful with pre-school children and should be preserved and continued into formal schooling. This, he maintains, would entail some key factors :

> i)   the child being at the centre of his learning wanting and needing to communicate;
> ii)   the child learns through interaction with his immediate environment, including people, things and animals;
> iii) the processes of learning not only include such behaviours as interaction, observation, experiment, experience, cause and effect; but also symbolic forms such as story, play, rhyme, lyric, song, dance, painting, myths, legends, imaginings;
> iv)   in addition to mother tongue learning in this model the child will also acquire knowledge about human nature; how people behave, how to gain reward, the consequences of certain behaviours   (based on) Neelands, 1992, pp.12-13).

Social and cultural contexts

Drama allows the teacher to transform his or her classroom so that concrete and real-life language contexts can be created and presented to the pupils. Dramatic role playing will enable both teacher and pupils to imagine they are in a variety of roles, in a variety of places faced with a variety of dilemmas, problems or issues. In other words the social context in which talk can take place is open to a range of new possibilities whereby participants in the action of a lesson can explore, experiment and practise with different audiences, purposes, content and styles.

It is often this social context and the appropriateness of speech which is most perplexing and confusing for young people, so much so that many youngsters in some ways regress and become withdrawn and unwilling communicators. This is associated with a number of interrelated factors which are as much to do with natural growth and puberty as they are with any psychological damage. However, to develop positive relationships, which are governed by status, gender, class and cultural background, is not always easy for the pupils in our schools. Selecting the appropriate form of discourse is a necessary and complex skill for everyday life. The demands of personal and domestic relationships need to be distinguished from the related but distinctive challenges of the world of work and/or life in the community if young people are to operate effectively in different environments.

Role play provides opportunities to establish a range of contexts for talk in the form of 'imagined experience' (Neelands, *op. cit.*). The activities, tasks and exercises outlined in this chapter are intended to give participants opportunities to play roles by projecting themselves into fictitious situations and to assume stances, opinions and feelings that are not necessarily their own. At times this may require experimenting with the attitudes of others or it may require imagining oneself in a different set of circumstances. Often it will call for attempts at realism but does not require the theatrical skills associated with the specifics of characterisation. The concern here is more to do with attitudes where pupils can be encouraged to adopt a stance towards a particular issue or to express a point of view or to experiment with solutions to problems and dilemmas.

The practical ideas are intended to be accessible and attractive to all teachers irrespective of phase or subject specialism. At times the role play element of a lesson may be brief and used to illustrate a teaching point; on other occasions role playing may be used in an extended project designed to explore a number of issues. The outcomes of the work will be specific to particular programmes but these may include some or all of the following learning for pupils:

> Help them to gain confidence, in a reasonably secure situation.
> Show them that their ideas will be accepted and used.
> Allow them to gain practice in adopting different attitudes.
> Give them practice in using varying levels of language.
> Give them practice in negotiating with other people.
> Give them practice in problem-solving, decision-making and situation-resolving.
> Show them that thoughtful examination of the activity will follow.
> Establish that 'showing the work' is not necessary.
> Give them practice in coping with new situations.
> O'Neill 1976 p.61).

All these skills are crucial to the ability of children with SEN, especially when these are emotional or behavioural, to cope with those situations where hasty or unconsidered action leads to conflict with others. The techniques advocated by Tutt (1978) for the examination of the triggers of anti-social or illegal activity in Intermediate Treatment settings are reminiscent of these activities.

Still images

The following ideas are based on the recognition that there are alternative modes of expression and forms of understandings to the verbal and literary modes. Indeed 'The Arts in Schools' project team reminds us that:

> The many different cultural forms of the arts emerge from the following elemental modes of understanding:
> • the visual mode - using light, colour and images
> • the aural mode - using sounds and rhythm
> • the kinaesthetic mode - using bodily movement
> • the verbal mode - using spoken or written words
> • the enactive mode - using imagined roles.
> (NCC 1990, pp..5-6)

Advocacy, and in particular self-advocacy, may therefore be best approached through a fuller use of this range of modes of understanding and forms of expression so that young people are given the opportunity to experiment with a variety of means for communication. In this respect the visual and enactive modes present alternative possibilities for the teacher without discarding or undermining the importance of other forms. In many respects it is impossible to separate the connections between all modes of understanding; however emphasis may be given to particular skills in particular programmes and these activities will be seen to have a distinctive drama (enactive) orientation. The initial approach, here, to advocacy and self-advocacy is suggested through the use of the familiar and accessible visual images.

Encounters with images through picture books, comics, photographs, paintings, posters, statues and toys can be used as sources of information and stimulation. Pupils' knowledge and expertise of still images will provide raw material and reference points for these activities. Using their own bodies pupils can be encourage to create individually, and collectively, 3D versions of sculptures, wax works, pictures, TV freeze frames and the like. Living tableaux have a number of advantages, not least those outlined by Fleming (1994, p. 93):

> The task culminates in silent, concentrated and focused work and is thus an attractive option from the point of view of control. It demands, and often promotes, group cohesion, and allows everyone to participate in some way whatever their level of skill or confidence. From the point of view of the teacher who is new to drama it is a valuable activity because, although a technique which can be usefully employed within a drama, it can also be used on its own as a one off exercise.

Statues

Freezing as a game and a natural extension to play is a useful starting point for young children but can be equally effective with older pupils if handled well. The teacher may begin by means of his or her own examples of freezes which can be guessed at by the class. Statues not only give factual information in terms of names, jobs, domestic chores, historical significance, etc. but can also convey inner feelings of sadness, joy, satisfaction, despair. Some initial demonstrations by the teacher will put the class at ease. A teacher in role as a visitor to a museum, historical site or formal garden will be able to join in a drama which in turn gives the class the opportunity to adopt a variety of freezes as they become statues in the appropriate setting. A simple narrative may allow the teacher (visitor) to comment indirectly on the statues created by the class: 'I think this statue would go very well in my new museum','What a spooky garden this is!', 'This statue shows what a kind person Florence Nightingale was', 'Oh, what an unusual piece of modern art!'

Groups too could be asked to create sculptured images; one group member may be given responsibility for positioning and arranging the statues to achieve the best effect. The brief given to pupils may call for a recreation of a known work of art, or to commemorate an historical event or celebrate a significant stage in local, national or global life. Older pupils might be called upon to prepare depictions based on more abstract ideas. These images can be read and interpreted by the class with an appropriate level of support by the teacher; alternatively a group member may act as a museum guide or artist who must explain the background and meaning to the sculpture. Those pupils with more confidence may be able to respond to questions posed by the class as visitors to the museum or tourists in the cathedral. Perhaps the teacher in role as curator, archbishop or minister of arts could make very specific demands on the pupil who acts as guide or artist, challenging the pupil in role to make a defence for a particular piece of sculpture, e.g. 'Why should the tax-payer buy this so called piece of art?', or 'Where could this go in my new hotel?' In this way this visual mode provides an opportunity for enactive and verbal modes of understanding; in many respects the pressure is taken off- whilst pupils focus on the visual aspects, they are indirectly engaging in those processes of self-expression which otherwise pose difficulties or cause inhibitions.

Wax works

The creation of human models is another device that allows pupils to demonstrate in groups, or as individuals, how stillness, gesture and facial expression can convey a range of ideas that combine informative and affective elements. Thematic approaches can be taken here whereby the class are asked to create different rooms in a wax works museum. Ideas based on actual visits or second-hand knowledge of wax works in theme parks and Madame Tussaud's will produce ideas such as a sports room, or an Elizabethan room, or a music room, or the chamber of horrors. However, the teacher may be able to develop this into areas that both further challenge pupils and allow them to express more personal and emotional aspects. A 'happiness' room might be one possibility, not merely reproducing figures with smiling faces, but attempting to encourage pupils to focus on the portrayal of positive incidents from their experience. Another idea based on Orwell's 'room 101' (or the theme of nightmares), could help pupils to explore and confront their fears. The teacher will need to judge if explanations are or are not appropriate and to what extent discussion should be encouraged.

Photographs

From an early age pupils have direct experience of photographs through family albums, newspapers and magazines. Here group photographs can begin to exploit pupils' knowledge and enthusiasms by asking for sports team photographs indicating, for example, particular sports, e.g. hockey, football, tennis; equipment, e.g. rackets, helmets, padding; roles, e.g. captain, coach, physio. But once again the affective domain can be introduced through the portrayal of success or failure, or perhaps there is animosity within the team that is captured in the photograph, or perhaps one team member is beginning to lose interest and wants to leave. The task now becomes a question of how photographs convey mood, atmosphere and internal motivations.

These themes can be explored using the concept of a family album. In different group sizes the joys, pains, tensions, changes and disappointments of family life become the focus of single moments in time. The physical nature of the activity and the distance drama lends to this work may allow pupils to experience, safely, memories, present difficulties, imaginings and hopes and fears for their future. Happy holiday snaps, birthday parties, weddings and various 'rites of passage', moments of mourning at the passing of loved ones are possibilities. Stages in personal and collective experience can provide opportunities for teacher and pupils to explore those common feelings and emotional bonds that give us all our common humanity; they are also opportunities for pupils to begin to express their ideas in relation to these important areas.

A further development could lie in the introduction of still photography to this style of work, using either a Polaroid camera for instant results or, more realistically, a conventional camera allowing time for development and printing. Teenage magazines frequently use the convention of photo-stories whereby a narrative is presented using a combination of photographs of real actors, real settings and a comic strip format. Through the photocopied versions of pre-staged photographs, cut and paste dialogue balloons and thought bubbles, pupils can plan, rehearse, shoot and present their stories. These photo-stories show pupils in roles facing dilemmas and problems that might otherwise cause embarrassment or require acting skills beyond their abilities. Here dialogue appears in a 'balloon' and innermost feelings can be conveyed in a 'bubble'; live acting is not necessary.

Record sleeves, CD covers and music posters are yet another medium that teenagers, in particular, are usually excited by. These images (often in the form of photo-montage) attempt to respond to the abstract qualities and personal content of the music. Musicians and singers become role models and even spokespersons for young people; some have been hailed as the 'voice of a generation'. In this sense advocacy may be supported through the ideas and style of a rock musician or rap group, becoming powerful symbols and effective channels of expression for young people. Pupils may therefore be inclined to capture emotional responses evoked by particular pieces of music through a still image (or collection of images) for an imagined poster that could become a means of communication in itself. Subsequent explanations, questioning and discussion may also be part of the teacher's intended learning.

Book illustrations

In the context of school, but sadly not in all homes, young people will have had plentiful opportunities for access to books, thereby engaging with both literary and visual text. To suggest that children with SEN lack such access may be thought to be stereotyping. However, it is certainly the case that many families, for cultural, social or financial reasons, may not encourage it.

Using living tableaux to replicate book illustrations allows the pupils to focus less on surface features such as narrative and action (although this can be a valid use of the convention when concepts associated with plot and sequence are deemed important), but more on sub-textual qualities such as motivation, tension, mood and atmosphere. Attention to details such as groupings, spacing, body language and gesture, can reveal a great deal about the emotional content of particular scenes. This may also be an appropriate form to introduce elements of speaking and listening in a presentational manner and in so doing prepare the way for further role playing. For example, characters in a scene can be given a signal (a tap on the shoulder, a request from the audience) to speak in role revealing inner thoughts and personal dilemmas; an elementary form of soliloquy in effect. The notion of 'pop-up' books could also add some key movements to the tableau in the form of a significant gesture, perhaps a hand shake, or a turn of the head, or a kiss, or a knife in the back. On given signals from the teacher (perhaps pretending to pull and push the page tab) one or more characters in the illustration can repeat these basic but significant movements.

The use of tableau in the form of book illustrations and the other techniques of still images enables the teacher to initiate drama activity and introduce the idea of adopting a role in a controlled, flexible and non-threatening manner. It can be used to develop an understanding of narrative and to focus on a particular moment of significance. Literature and story, myth and legend, rhyme and poetry can therefore be used in preparatory phases leading to more extended and explicit sequences of dramatic role playing. It is to this strategy that attention now turns.

Beginning role play

Alfie has had an eventful evening; the class have just heard the teacher read about the burst water pipe in Alfie's house (Hughes, 1984). The baby sitter, Maureen, did not know what to do, there was water everywhere, Annie-Rose (Alfie's baby sister) woke up and Maureen's mum and dad had to come to help. It is now the next morning in Alfie's house, the teacher has put the book aside and is pretending to be Alfie's dad getting breakfast. A pupil has volunteered to be Alfie and whilst miming eating corn flakes he is retelling (with gentle prompts from the teacher) the story of the night before to his dad who has now joined Alfie at the breakfast table. This exercise covers much the same ground that a question and answer session with the class would also cover; here the class are involved in this conversation, they listen intently and many are also keen to have a turn at being Alfie. Later they will take turns to be Alfie's mum on the phone to a busy plumber who is unwilling to make a house call to fix the burst pipe. Practice with transactional language, yes; but also an opportunity for pupils to show frustration, persuasive skills, good humour, or anxiety.

A key strategy here is that of teacher-in-role, pioneered by Dorothy Heathcote (Johnson and O'Neill, 1984; Wagner, 1976) , whereby the teacher has now entered the drama alongside her class so that she can manage the drama from within the action. In this way the teacher is able to model enthusiasm and commitment to the activity whilst also being in a position to exploit a number of learning possibilities. This strategy allows teachers and pupils to lay aside their normal roles and enables both parties to work with the implications of new relationships which will include different levels of status and responsibilities. Pupils who have difficulty in accepting the authority of teachers or those who are intimidated by the normal control structures of our schools may find a certain liberation in these new roles.

However, the teacher does not enter the drama completely freely, but will still retain aims and objectives in terms of the pupils' learning which will need consideration when choosing the type of role to be adopted. The function of the role will have both dramatic implications and educative possibilities. For example, Morgan and Saxton, (1987) are able to list nine examples of roles that might be adopted by teachers, giving also the status, stance, description, advantages, disadvantages, potential learning and finally practical examples for each one The roles indicated range from 'Authority' to 'Second in Command', through to 'One of the Gang' and 'The Helpless'.

Teachers who initially feel uncomfortable with this technique will often adopt an authority role, e.g. Queen, Captain, Chief which in effect has many similarities to their normal classroom role. An intermediary role can be useful in that more responsibility is given to the class. Here the teacher can refer to a higher authority, e.g. 'I will have to ask her majesty about that', or 'The boss says three workers will have to be made redundant by the end of the week.' Dorothy Heathcote made much use of teacher-in-role strategies in generating dramatic experiences for young people with severe learning difficulties, and has been asked particularly to introduce difficult subjects, such as relationships, responsibility, and even scientific concepts, to such students. Yet it is also important to remember that teacher-in-role is only one technique among many for encouraging role play.

> It is quite possible to teach drama without this technique and
> indeed it is better to do so if there are major reservations about its
> use; pupils are quick to detect uncertainty and will not believe in
> the role if the teacher lacks confidence. As with other techniques
> it is one which can be overused with the result that pupils are
> given insufficient initiative for planning, advancing and shaping
> the drama (even with the adoption of a minor part, teacher in role
> is very influential). On the other hand, used appropriately, it is
> one of the most powerful techniques available to the teacher.
> Fleming 1994, p.99).

The strategy of 'hot seating' or questioning in role could be a more gentle way-in for both teacher and pupils; treated in the manner of a game it is a non-threatening introduction to adopting a role. For example the teacher, followed by volunteer pupils, can pretend to be a well-known personality who will answer 'Yes' or 'No' to questions from the class who are trying to guess the identity of the unknown visitor to the classroom. The advantage here is that the role player has little pressure in that simple answers only are required, but the technique can be developed into more sophisticated questioning and answering processes and more lengthy role playing sequences. It is a useful preparation for some of the more extensive role play suggestions which are to follow. Source material for the 'hot seated' roles can be derived from literature, e.g. how did Jack's mother feel whilst he was missing up the beanstalk? Or from history, e.g. questions addressed to a Viking or to a mill owner after a Factory Act. Or from material closer to pupils' own experiences, e.g. a shopkeeper whose business is next to a school or a mother learning that her teenage daughter is pregnant. Finally, the questioning may be given a specific context, e.g. the England football team manager at a press conference or a patient 'in the psychiatrist's chair'.

Working in pairs and groups

Scenarios that require interactive approaches are further possibilities for encouraging young people to find a voice through collaborative processes. Once again teachers may wish to introduce the work by using content that is grounded in pupils' own experience whilst at the same time retaining a protective distance. Borrowing sums of money, articles needed for school or items such as records, tapes, T-shirts, etc. can provide the starting point for more personal or significant requests. A simple role play based on borrowing £10 might provide opening material for a unit of work, covering a number of sessions that will not only give pupils the opportunity to interact with several different colleagues but will also allow pupils to comment directly or indirectly on their needs as part of a school community. In following this process some guidelines emerge for introducing role play. For example, initially interactions of a short duration are advisable, where possibly changing partners will facilitate social learning; changed partners will also enable pupils to rehearse their contributions a number of times. The principle of drafting and refining ones contributions is as important with spoken language as it is with written language.

In practice the process might progress through a number of stages beginning with the formation of a circle and the teacher demonstrating how he or she might go about borrowing a pair of training shoes for PE. The class could then be quickly divided into pairs by the teacher, who informs the pupils that they will be working with a number of different partners. As 'A' and 'B', each pair is given roles as lender and potential borrower. Each 'A' will be visited by each of three Bs who try to borrow £10; they must try to persuade the As that they have a good case. As will not decide to whom they will give the money until all three borrowers have been heard. Bs will move around the circle to a new partner once the teacher indicates time up; moving back in reverse order to hear the verdict from each A, who must justify their decision. After some light-hearted feedback to find out who received most money (failed attempts need not be made public), further reflection might focus on the need to consider how the manner in which we make requests often influences the outcome more than the actual nature of the request, in other words 'it ain't what you say, it's the way that you say it'. Para-linguistic considerations need to be made explicit: the significance of a smile, the negativity of certain aspects of body language are not always obvious to young people.

At this stage, or in the next session, it may be appropriate to reverse the roles allowing further opportunities to work with new partners and to rehearse these short informal interpersonal presentations. The request for £10 may become a request to copy a piece of homework; the roles of two friends may become teacher and pupil or teenager and parent but the persuasive nature of the interaction is retained- the communication of personal need is at the heart of the exercise, which may be relaxed or business-like, informal or competitive, depending on the group and the teacher's intentions.

The activity can be taken a stage further in its organisation and its content. Groups may now be formed with a more detailed brief, for example, they represent a charity (perhaps allocated by the teacher or self-selected by the group) and they are to visit a number of companies who are offering donations to selected charities, presenting a good case for receiving the funds. Alternatively, groups might be asked to consider their needs as a school, a class or group within the class who have an opportunity to apply for special funds or resources to support their particular requirements. If appropriate, the teacher may facilitate the preparation of these applications with a variety of source materials, presentational devices and equipment. Visitors, parents, other classes may be used in the role of donating companies or individuals who must consider the relative worth of the various applications. The merits of buying new football kit or providing facilities for the disabled or a video recorder for the Year 11 common room can be explored.

This style of role play development may focus on other areas of learning; rather than a financial topic and the language of persuasion being at the centre of the teacher's concerns, more imaginative topics and the language of description and narrative could be used to equal effect. Partners might initially exchange descriptions of their respective journeys to school. Moving around the circle and working with a number of different partners, these stories can be changed, added to and exaggerated until the seeds of an action/disaster movie emerge. Now in collaboration with a partner, pupils play the roles of screen writers presenting their 'treatment' and/or storyboard of the eventful journey to a group of Hollywood producers played by the teacher and the rest of the class when not making their own presentation. Here pupils are given a context in which they are expected and encouraged to give voice to their imaginations and fantasies. The audience also has a role to play and may be expected to ask relevant questions. After all, the rise of Quentin Tarantino from video shop assistant to 'Reservoir Dogs' and 'Pulp Fiction' has probably not gone un-noticed by most teenagers.

The nature of evidence and inquiry skills can also be explored using a similar structure. The initial roles will now be police officers taking statements from witnesses in relation to a crime or incident, organised again as pair work in a class circle. This may give the teacher an opportunity to allow pupils to explore controversial content areas whilst ensuring the work does not become threatening or too personal, e.g. racism, theft, family histories. Police officers can be checked for the accuracy of their memory and their listening skills. As a development, working in pairs, pupils can be given time to prepare alibis whilst other teams of pupils, acting as detectives, will prepare questions and organise a space to simulate an interrogation room (Sweeney and Catt, 1993). A police context is often appealing to young people who are knowledgeable about police procedures through watching popular TV programmes and listening to the playground grapevine. Presenting young people with these activities can encourage individuals to experiment with their thoughts and feelings concerning the topics; the team work involved also begins to help pupils to understand themselves and their reactions to others. An important feature of the work should also be the evaluation and reflective discussions that follow, where, if appropriate, teachers can tackle issues, problems and personal concerns at a more explicit level. The protective qualities of the role and the fictional context can be discarded in order to confront groups and individuals with what may at times be harsh realities. Needless to say, this requires sensitive judgements on behalf of the teacher and a good knowledge of the teaching group. This should be borne in mind as we explore further possibilities for role play in the classroom.

Role plays with 'split briefs'

Once a class becomes familiar with the basic techniques of role play - the adoption of roles, sustaining a fictional interaction and developing alternative standpoints within a given context - it is possible to introduce a different format to the proceedings. Not only will this add variety and hopefully encourage interest and motivation, but it also enables the teacher to develop more detailed interactions. The use of separate instructions or 'split briefs' for those playing different roles gives the teacher the opportunity to provide the role players with the appropriate information to play the role in sufficient depth. For young children this background information may be concise and very basic but for older children or for those who are able and confident in their ability to adopt and sustain a role, the brief could be extensive, detailed and requiring extra personal research undertaken by the role players themselves. At this level the brief or set of instructions will usually be written and given to each role player to look at, absorb and integrate into their acting as they feel appropriate. However, taped instructions can also be used to good effect; this way the teacher can brief several groups with separate instructions whilst remaining in control of the whole class.

It is vital that the instructions for each role are only seen by those playing that particular role. Otherwise, the sense of unpredictability and spontaneity which is an important ingredient in this approach will be lost. It may not be necessary to brief all role players at the same time; for example, whilst half a class of infants are sat on chairs spaced around the hall acting the role of a Queen/King on a throne, anxious about the preparations for the forthcoming royal wedding, the other half of the class are listening to the teacher at one end of the hall informing them that in their role as Lord Chancellor they must explain to this bad tempered monarch that the wedding cannot go ahead because the Queen's/King's daughter has run away.

As classes develop confidence they will be able to cope with more detailed instructions and will use the brief prepared by the teacher as a starting point from which they will develop and add their own ideas. A typical example of this approach to role play might replicate the following format and will include background information given to all pupils and separate instructions given to individual role players.

The Suitcase
Characters
A - Father/mother
B - Only son/daughter (your age)
Situation
A and B have not been getting on very well recently. It is about 9 o' clock one evening when A goes into B's room and finds B putting things into a suitcase. A cannot see exactly what B is doing because B hurriedly shuts the case and pushes it under the bed. B stands up and is clearly very embarrassed.
Setting
A room with a bed, one chair, one entrance. Something to represent a suitcase.
Organisation
Cast the parts.
Arrange the working space as you want it.
Read your separate instructions, but do not discuss them.
A - B has been secretive lately and you are worried about this. You are also concerned about the fact that B has been coming in late in the evenings. You want to have a talk about all this, so you go to B's room. When you open the door your first impression is that B has decided to leave home secretly.
B - You are beginning to feel hemmed in by life at home. A has been nagging you and prying into your private life. On the other hand you have been feeling irritable and tired, too, so maybe it is partly your fault. You have decided to try to make things up and so have bought A a present. You have hidden it in a suitcase, which you have stuck under your bed. You were just getting the present out to wrap it up, when A came into your room - snooping again?

Starting Point
B is kneeling by the suitcase , back to door.
A opens the door and walks in.
(Seely, 1978, p.2)

Using this or a similar format, teachers will soon be able to adapt published materials or begin to write their own role plays in order to focus on issues or topics that are of concern to their classes. History teachers will be able to include relevant data when preparing an encounter between an evacuee from 1940s London and a welcoming rural family. Likewise, an RE lesson or a science lesson might include a role play on an ethical issue which will contain detailed briefs given to different protagonists who must voice the appropriate arguments. For some children who find it difficult to articulate their own views, or who have not yet formulated their own views on a particular subject, this approach enables them to use the brief to propose a case, to put forward an argument. They become involved in the process of debate albeit at second hand, but nevertheless, for these young people the interaction is important in itself and lays a foundation for a more personal response at a later date.

Role plays involving larger numbers organised on similar lines also provide opportunities for interactions with an added dynamic provided by the fact that each participant in the role play does not know exactly how the others have been briefed and therefore can only guess at how the others are going to react. In this respect the role play attempts to mirror real experience. The briefing process also allows groups of participants playing the same role to collaborate in their preparation. At a basic level this might simply mean an able pupil is giving the task of reading the brief to the others. In more co-operative preparatory phases, pupils will be able to discuss with each other how they intend to play the part. This will enable less confident and less articulate pupils to hear what colleagues intend to say, what gestures they might use, what tone of voice could be appropriate. The teacher will need to guard against this becoming a recipe for uniformity as opposed to a genuine collaboration which is a necessary preparatory stage prior to a personal attempt to play their allocated role.

Out-of-role discussion is also possible at intervals during a role play where the teacher will stop a scene at a chosen point, putting the action on 'hold', whilst participants re-group with those from other groups playing the same role. This will enable pupils to give each other progress reports and to get ideas from each other. Support is therefore available to those who may need it within a collaborative framework rather than as remedial help from the teacher. Again, this is a valuable strategy for providing support to less able pupils without drawing attention to the fact that some pupils are having difficulty in arguing their case. Once these informal conferences have taken place, roles are once again taken up and the action begins from where it was left off. One or two scenes can be 'spotlighted' for a brief time to allow other groups the opportunity to eavesdrop on the action before continuing with their own scenes. This begins to introduce a theatrical aspect to the process, albeit without the accompanying pressures of re-arranging chairs for an audience, or organising entrances and exits. It allows for presentational elements to be eased into the work in non-threatening ways.

'Forum theatre'

The activities suggested so far have emphasised the active involvement of participants in taking roles and expressing points of view through fictional circumstances. Out-of-role discussion has also been highlighted and in many respects it is during this reflective talk that many pupils develop insight into themselves and their particular circumstances. These processes have to a large extent avoided overtly theatrical forms of presentation; the presence of spectators has not been encouraged in any formal sense although the concept of audience is important in all these speaking and listening activities. However, the reproduction of a role play in front of an audience can present the teacher with opportunities to encourage young people to comment on what they witness as spectators and to indicate how they feel the drama reflects their own experiences, feelings and views about how things happen or should happen.

In this form of theatre the action can be stopped by members of the audience when they feel misrepresentations emerge or when the authenticity of the portrayed events is threatened. At this point suggestions can be given to the actors, information may be supplied or opinions put forward by members of the audience, who may disagree between themselves about the issues and events in question. Different versions of a problem may be presented; members of the audience may wish to take over a particular role to show their side of the story. With young children this may focus on imaginary events so that pupils may experiment with the best way to approach the princess who has run away from home. In one version of the narrative, the princess may refuse to return to the castle to be married but after various attempts by different emissaries she may finally be persuaded by a particular argument.

For older pupils more realistic dramas may cover similar issues of protest, injustice, sexual relations. Dramas can be devised to portray particular incidents of racial or sexual harassment which may provide opportunities for pupils not only to express points of view but also to show colleagues how things feel or how things can be changed. Hence the role of the audience becomes much more dynamic and participative. This form of role playing will often generate debate and controversy which, if handled well, will stimulate young people to express their views and opinions.

'Committees of inquiry'

Class discussions of controversial and sensitive issues are not always easy to manage. The teacher is often confronted with young people who are formulating views and opinions but are having to do this whilst undergoing physical and emotional developments which greatly influence their responses. This will cause some to dominate, some to be aggressive, some to act the clown, some to shock and others who will take a passive role. Handling this range of reactions within the heightened atmosphere of many of our classrooms is difficult and a range of strategies are needed. Whilst not wishing to forsake the opportunities for personal contributions that a well conducted class discussion will provide, it may be necessary to avoid a free-wheeling debate in favour of more formal approaches. The organisation of committees of inquiry is one way of doing this whilst not losing the creative edge that role play can bring to this type of work.

Encouraging young people to see two sides to a story, to appreciate the views of others, to consider the whole picture, is an important part of their development. This is often difficult when tackled in the abstract or when presented in the form of materials to be read and evaluated before making a personal response, be it written or verbal. Using role play to present evidence from a number of angles gives young people the chance to interact with the information at a more human level. The procedures of committees of inquiry can be helpful models in that these committees interview witnesses, seek informed opinion and challenge conjecture before making a recommendation or suggesting a course of action.

It is possible to replicate this in the classroom in a way which uses many of the activities suggested so far in this chapter. For example, presenting the class with the dilemma of dealing with a fictitious pupil with a history of disruptive behaviour. Karen is such a girl who, having a history of disruption on day visits, now wants to go on a school residential trip. Should she be allowed to go?

Her teachers are divided; Mr Ormerod, in charge of the trip, supports her application; Mr Hardy, her year head, thinks she should be banned. Sandra, an influential pupil in the same year, also thinks she should remain in school (Davis and Long, 1983, pp..49-55). Four pupils can be asked to take on these roles and are given appropriate briefs to support their acting. These briefs are studied by the four actors who ensure their background details are not read by the others. The rest of the class are formed into four committees of inquiry who will interview each witness before making a recommendation. Once the interviews are complete and the recommendations published and/or explained verbally, further class discussion may then result.

Here the human dimension to these dilemmas and problems is highlighted through role play but it may also provide teachers and pupils with the opportunity to put their case through using a character and a role as their mouthpiece. Once again the fictional context creates a safety net for pupils to experiment with finding their voice without the fear of falling too far. Difficult and controversial topics such as crime and punishment, serious illness, birth control, abortion, can be explored using this structured approach.

Conclusion

In conclusion, the suggestions outlined are intended to provide stimulus to those teachers wishing to explore drama as a medium for learning. Pupils with special educational needs are entitled to a say in the way their world is shaped, both in school and the wider community. Without confidence and communicative power they will find it difficult to express their ideas, desires and feelings in constructive ways. Drama, through its unique blend of imagined experience and social learning, provides the vital ingredients for young people to explore and experiment with these concepts, attitudes and skills. Through the creative processes of role taking and role playing difficulties, can be set aside and/or overcome to give pupils with SEN the opportunity to find their voice and to let it be heard.

PUPIL PARTICIPATION IN THE SOCIAL AND EDUCATIONAL PROCESSES OF A PRIMARY SCHOOL

Jacquie Coulby and David Coulby

Introduction

This chapter is concerned with three themes: self-advocacy, pupil behaviour and the management of a primary school. At the primary phase, 'pupil participation' might provide a less jargonised equivalent for self-advocacy. The bulk of the chapter is concerned with strategies to encourage the participation of young children in the running of their own school lives. The reference to children with special educational needs here is direct rather than tangential. The school which we describe has its fair share of children formally and informally perceived to have such needs, and they form part of this chapter. But the real relevance of what we describe to the schooling of children perceived to have special educational needs lies in our assumption that such needs are actually generated within classrooms and schools. Pupil behaviour and the management of the primary school are themes which we have previously attempted to connect (Coulby, J. and Coulby, D. 1990). The vast majority of children perceived to have special needs are those who have engaged in behaviour in school which teachers and headteachers have found unacceptable. The bureaucratic and pseudo-scientific procedures and belief systems whereby this lack of acceptance of behaviour is formalised into the various categories of 'need' in order to legitimate exclusion have been thoroughly described elsewhere (Tomlinson, 1981; 1982). In seeking to reduce the number of children subjected to these procedures we have sought ways of both reducing the amount of pupil behaviour likely to be considered unacceptable and of encouraging teachers to consider critically the boundaries of what they are prepared to accept. It is a truism that the majority of special needs work takes place in mainstream schools: it should be equally obvious that the majority of this work is concerned with prevention.

Self-advocacy, then, is a third theme which might be seen to sit uneasily with the first two. If the theory and practice is that by generating appropriate managerial, pedagogical and curricular systems then the incidence of both learning and behaviour difficulties can be dramatically reduced, then what space does this give to student individuality in any form? The question is all the sterner when it concerns children of primary school age. Self-advocacy with young adults could itself be seen as part of a management system designed just as much to control as to liberate. Few primary school age children lack individuality. Indeed the systems approach to learning and behaviour difficulties which we have repeatedly advocated might be seen as an organised way of constraining - to use no harsher word - such individualism in the interests of social control and intellectual conformity. Self-advocacy or pupil participation is a necessary third category for two important reasons. Firstly, the systems we describe are not designed to engender either academic or behavioural conformity. On the contrary, they are designed to allow all pupils to fulfil their potential and to prevent them being exposed to the processes and institutions of segregation. Secondly, if these systems were imposed by teachers on young pupils they would not work anyway. It is the harsh imposition of arbitrary systems - admittedly somewhat different from those we advocate - which in the past has encouraged pupil resistance and nonconformity with the associated negative educational results for all concerned. If pupils are placed at the centre of the social and educational processes of the primary school then the resulting systems will not be something imposed upon them but rather the institutionalisation of their own self-development. If the children are involved in the formulation and modification of the maximum number of aspects of these systems then they will have a much greater potential to be liberating as well as successful.

Self-advocacy or pupil participation is an essential part of a primary education which seeks to minimise the number of pupils whose needs are formally found to be 'special'. More portentously, pupil participation is an essential element of a primary education in a democratic society. The remainder of this chapter is divided into four sections: behaviour policy and ethos;

democracy and individualism; involvement of pupils and parents in the school curriculum and special needs.

Batheaston CEVC Primary is a medium sized school serving a socially mixed locality on the fringe of the city of Bath. The children are aged from 4 to 11. There is a Playgroup closely connected to the school and located in one of its rooms but there is no nursery. The policies and practices which we describe below are by no means unique to this school, but they form part of a unified approach to learning and behaviour which is widely supported by teachers, non-teaching staff and parents.

Behaviour policy and ethos

These two items are treated together since they are inseparable and central elements of school policy. The school has an explicit *Behaviour Policy*, a document designed to share strategies with those such as students or supply teachers who are temporarily attached to the school. The children know that all the staff care about them and their behaviour. *All* staff therefore make it their responsibility to know all the children and to have a response to anything they come across. Similarly all staff are equally valued, teaching and non-teaching staff alike and all are committed to the educational and social life of the school. All staff are used to reward good achievement - children frequently go and show other teachers, the cook, the secretary, etc. a good piece of work. Other children are also told about things of which a particular class feels proud, such as a wall display, and are invited in to see it. Once a week, children's work is shared with the whole school in a special assembly. A check is kept that all children's good work is shown regularly, and the other children are invited to come to classes to see displays and presentations. When a child has made a significant improvement or produced a really special piece of work then this may feature in a badge assembly (see the next section) and/or result in a letter acknowledging the achievement being sent home to parents (see Figure 1).

Social mixing across age groups is encouraged. When the 4-year olds start school they are matched with a special friend. These are generally the 9 and 10-year olds. They collect the younger children and take them out to play; they usually organise games for them; help them to mix; help them with coats, etc. They also go to lunch with them when they first stay and help them to get their food; they collect them and take them to assemblies, where they sit with them, explaining things and helping them to listen quietly. This experience provides responsibility for the older children as well as assistance, friendship and a role model for the younger ones.

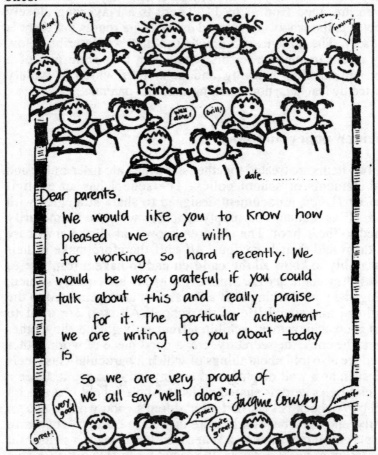

Figure 1: Congratulations!

Children are encouraged to be involved in the process of behaviour management. The children are encouraged to observe and identify appropriate 'good' behaviour and to praise each other. They are involved in developing the school and class rules (see below, Figure 2).Their ideas are sought in particular problem-solving sessions. The difficulties of individual children in terms of learning and/or behaviour are talked about openly, seen as temporary, and children who help with these are specifically praised and thanked. Children are treated respectfully and spoken to politely. If ever something goes wrong, the inappropriate responses/behaviour are identified through individual/group discussion, alternative strategies identified, solutions/apologies worked out and, if necessary, sanctions enforced. If the misdeed is significant the parents are contacted and involved in the discussions or sanctions.

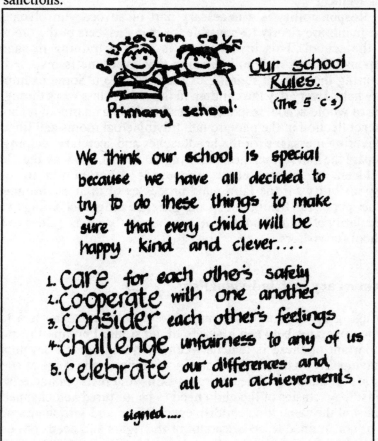

Figure 2 : School rules

A variety of opportunities, such as role play and assemblies are used to help children develop strategies for difficult group situations such as how to say 'no' when the rest of a group say 'yes' (to a cigarette, for instance) or how to respond as a group to unfriendly or unsporting playground behaviour. Assemblies are frequently used in this way: they provide the children with a training in self-presentation, debate and self-articulation. High expectations of behaviour and the commitment for learning for all children are linked to a differentiated curriculum and specific attention to learning difficulties. Central to the school's approach is the identification, appreciation and reward of good work and behaviour. This focuses on effort and attitude as well as on achievement.

Responsibility is a necessary part of advocacy/involvement. The pupils are clearly responsible for many aspects of the running of the school. This involvement is itself a training in shared responsibility as well an indication that everyone is involved in ensuring the smooth running of the institution. Some examples may help. Every day the children in the oldest class work through a rota of whole-school responsibilities for about a quarter of an hour: litter collection in the playground, tidying cloakrooms and library, delivering messages for the headteacher and secretary, helping to prepare the hall for lunches, watering plants. In this way the older children are motivated to encourage other pupils to take responsibility for the fabric and processes of their environment. Other pupils run the tuck shop and generate orders according to the popularity of items. Pupils of all ages regularly act as guides to the school for visitors.

Democracy and individualism

Bringing up children either as a parent or as a teacher is a task which operates between a series of tensions. Perhaps the most important of these is that between encouraging and developing individuality on the one hand and inculcating a wide range of social norms on the other. The emerging skills, interests, characteristics and idiosyncrasies of the child need to be nurtured and channelled whilst at the same time childish egocentrism and selfishness need to be constrained to take account of the rights and needs of peers, of adults, of institutions and occasions (traffic, mealtimes), and of wider society. Put in different terms, this is the tension between individualism and self-direction, each with its potential for competition and conflict, on the one hand and cooperation on the other. To err on one side is to encourage solipsistic individualism; to err on the other is to insist on institutional and social conformity. Elsewhere (Bash *et al.*, 1985) we have made a distinction between socialisation and social control to attempt to elaborate this tension.

However, it is obviously always a matter of balance which each parent or school must attempt to maintain with each child.

For a primary school even to have a behaviour policy is for it to stress one side of this balance. But without such a policy a school is likely to encourage behaviours which will ultimately limit the learning possibilities and indeed the opportunities for individual development of all pupils. The paradox is that without some support for social and individual norms it is impossible to create an atmosphere and an environment in which individual learning and growth can occur. Character is not disarticulated from society and its institutions: rather it is shaped within them. It is the extent of this shaping which is the delicate matter of professional balance. The section above dealt with institutional behaviour policy. Within that policy for control it is clear that there are stresses on equality and individuality. This section outlines those aspects of the school's policy which also seek to maintain that side of the balance. It is within this section that policies which most closely connect with those associated with involvement/self-advocacy are likely to be found. In the terms of this chapter, these policies are concerned with the involvement of individual children in the school and of the school in individual children. These policies are only possible against a background of clear expectations for equality and opportunities for daily group discussion and constant modelling by adults of responsibility and participation.

The school operates to a firm policy of equality. This applies to the familiar categories of race, gender and class, but also to those perceived or categorised as having special educational needs (see below).

Issues of status as between teaching and non-teaching staff, staff and parents and indeed staff and pupils are minimised wherever this is possible. Parents and ancillaries work independently alongside teachers in both classrooms and playground. Children refer to all staff by their first names. (This policy has not been controversial with parents or the community though at one point it generated considerable hysterical copy in the local newspaper.) The products of the children are seen to permeate in the management and presentation of the school. The school logo was chosen from a competition of the designs of children at the school.

As well as being a statement of cooperation and equality, it is clearly the product of a child.

It features prominently on the school's official notepaper, on school uniform and on official documents such as the prospectus. It semiotically asserts the primacy of the children in the structures and identity of the school.

In more formal democratic terms there is a School Council (for a recent, national account of how these can work see Haigh, 1994). This consists of two elected representatives from each class who meet with the headteacher once a term. Obviously the Council in no sense controls the school. However, the following account of one meeting is an indication of the extent to which children can participate in the formation of decisions which influence their everyday lives. We quote these minutes in full since they also give an insight into the way in which behaviour policies are arbitrated and implemented in order to ensure the maximum consensus and support. They also indicate that even the youngest children can participate actively at this level, bringing items to the agenda as well as participating in the discussion.

MINUTES OF COUNCILLORS' MEETING
Tuesday, 19th April

1.   Uniform Everyone felt they did want a uniform and some felt it should be obligatory. We discussed how we could not actually insist on it. The Councillors felt that we should encourage it.

Wearing denim was discussed and it was to be OK if SMART (not old), and new and dark. We all agreed there was a problem with Y6, whose parents were saving to get a new school uniform for Secondary School. We decided we should encourage everyone to wear it, and if they couldn't manage all of it, at least to get a navy or red top.

2.   Football The young children felt it was not fair that they could only play in the big playground. There had been lots of complaints. So, after much discussion, it was agreed that:
if damp, Class 5 and 6 mixed would play football in the top playground, with the rest of the school in the big playground; if dry, Class 5 and 6 would play football on the bottom grass. The rest of the school would have the top playground and top grass, and Classes 1, 2, 3 and 4 would have football in the big playground. PLEASE NOTE: Everyone felt that GIRLS CAN

PLAY FOOTBALL (even if they are not too good at it), and anyone in Class 5 or 6 can play. If anyone says 'you can't play football' they get banned for the rest of that day and the next day.

*3.   **New Arrangements** Alternative weeks table duty and eating list. So, eat first and do tables. Gemma, Luke, Anthony and Katie are to do the new rotas.*

*4.   **School Fund Friday Collection** A suggestion was made and taken up to get more playground equipment. Cake money and the Friday silver collection will go towards this.*

*5.   **Monitors for playground** Cathy would work out some monitors for all the playground equipment. Ideas of some things to get out to play with: cones, tunnels, hoola hoops, basketball ring and ball, high jump stands to use for goal posts, jacks. Ideas for designs/drawings on the playground: shadow clock, long jump, marked racing area on bottom playground or outside Class 6. We decided to ask children for donations of equipment - things for outside, cars, lego etc. It was requested that we put up mirrors in both loos. Everyone thought this an excellent idea.*

*6.   **Class 5** Class 5 had made lots of complaints about always being last for dinners. A solution was found: Class 5 and 6 will take it in turns, alternate weeks to eat first/last. On the week that they eat first, they will also clear away the hall. Everyone thought that this was a good idea and the Class 5 and 6 Councillors agreed to draw up the rotas. Jacquie said she would explain it to the lunchtime supervisors.*

*7.   **Playground Behaviour** Councillors felt that Class 6 sometimes taught the little ones rude words. Jacquie will speak to the children about this in assembly. Councillors said that karate and play fighting was seen by many as a nuisance and also some people felt left out. After discussion, the following was decided and Jacquie agreed to inform everyone at the next assembly (and to tell the lunchtime supervisors):*
1.   Karate and play fighting: From now on, this is totally banned. If people want to play in this way they should do so out of school. Anyone playing karate/fighting would be taken by the lunchtime supervisor to Jacquie and kept inside for a lunchtime as a reminder.

2. There will now be a ban on saying 'you can't play': From now on, if someone tells you can't play, we'd like you to tell the lunchtime supervisor who will talk it over with you and take the child who has said 'you can't play' to Jacquie, who will make them stay inside for a lunchtime. This includes the footballers and everyone else.

The meeting was then closed and councillors agreed to feed back all these agreements to the rest of the school in assembly.

The discussion and decisions here go a long way beyond tokenism. A further decision, which is linked to the uniform issue at the beginning of these minutes, may be used to reinforce this. When a noticeable number of children started to come to school wearing denim - which actually met the uniform requirement of being either red or navy - the issue was referred to the Parents' Voice group to ascertain their views. After much discussion this Group could not reach a clear decision so they in turn referred it to the School Council as the most appropriate point where advice could be offered. Further, the school recognises that pupils have their own priorities when it comes to the allocation of resources collected through fundraising. The School Council provides the forum in which these priorities can be itemised.

All but the oldest class operate a system of appointing a Special Person each day. This is mainly done by rota, but can be managed to match birthdays or difficulties such as an anxious child going to the dentist. The Special Person has certain enjoyable responsibilities - taking the register to the secretary, choosing children to line up and so on. In several classes, the Special Person is responsible for monitoring the noise level and reminding children if it is meant to be a particularly quiet time (the aim being for them all to gain experience of focusing on appropriate/convenient levels of noise as well as fulfilling the function of maintaining a quiet working atmosphere). At the end of their special day, the Special Person has to identify one or two people who have behaved in a friendly way: they are encouraged to describe *how*. They then award these children a sticker for friendly behaviour. The older children tend to discuss friendly behaviour slightly differently. They have a Child of the Week system. Each child in turn is the focus of class observation and discussion. The children are invited through the week to write on a wall chart the ways in which the Child of the Week has performed well, in terms of friendly, co-operative behaviour, work or attitude. The child in question also expresses any difficulties they have with behaviour at the beginning of the week, and their classmates offer suggestions and support. At the end of the week, they take their wall chart home to keep.

Another policy which balances between the development of individuality and the control of behaviour is that involving whole school badges. In this case the repertoire of desirable behaviours was evolved through staff discussion. Having agreed these, appropriate badges were made. Each class has three regular badges: 'I have done some beautiful work'; 'I have behaved very well'; 'I have done some excellent work'. Every week, the class teachers nominate children for these badges; the children can make nominations to the teachers. Each class teacher also chooses a few of the following general badges: 'I have tried extremely hard'; 'I have been very polite and cheerful'; 'I have completed all my work this week'; 'I have been extremely friendly and co-operative'; 'I have worked well with other children'; 'I have done some brilliant work'; 'I have made a big step forward'; 'I have done something very special'; 'I have made a tremendous achievement'; 'I have been really helpful'; 'I am good at homework'; 'I have been a star'; 'I have had some great ideas'; 'I have been really good at lunchtimes'. There is a weekly Badge Assembly. The aim is to keep a regular discussion going about what sorts of actions make up 'good' behaviour. The teachers write a covering sentence saying what the child has specifically done, for instance, *how* a child was co-operative to another child. The children value the badges and take them very seriously: parents, teachers and other children tend to praise the children wearing the badges for the week. Once again, teachers would ensure that *all* children received a badge sometimes.

School and class rules are also developed democratically. This process is described elsewhere (Coulby, J., 1986). The key elements at school level are: behaviour being an important topic of general discussion in all classes; children working out what rules are necessary to the safe and effective conduct of the school; the overarching framework is that there should be as few rules as possible and that they should all be phrased in a positive way; children work in small groups in class to evolve the appropriate rules; this process is then repeated at school level; when the list is finalised it is ratified by all the classes; the final formal list is signed by all the children and staff.

Involvement of pupils and parents in the school curriculum

Participation by both teachers and pupils in the formation of the school curriculum has been severely reduced by the introduction of the National Curriculum in the wake of the 1988 Education Act. The subjects to be studied and even the smallest details of topics and themes have, since then, been prescribed by central government for England and Wales. However, in the light of the government's acceptance of the Dearing proposals for radically slimming down the curriculum (Dearing,.1993a; 1993b; DFE 1993), there will soon be space in the primary school to teach knowledge beyond and different from that prescribed in the National Curriculum. Potentially this returns a great deal of autonomy to primary teachers and greatly increases the scope for pupil's involvement in their own education. Whilst it may not be possible for very young children to map out the knowledge and skills which they wish to acquire at school, if pupils have no say whatsoever in the curriculum, then they are likely to see knowledge as something inflicted on them without their choice or participation. Similarly parents often wish to have some say in what their child learns at school. This is very rarely a matter of attempting to constrain the curriculum, but stems from their knowledge of the strengths, weaknesses and progress of their particular child. Certainly if pupils and parents have no say in the actual business of the school or the curriculum, then it will be all the easier for them to become alienated and remote from the institution as a whole. This section explores some of the strategies whereby, within the confines of the National Curriculum, the primary school might seek to involve parents and pupils in curriculum planning.

In some ways to ask to what extent pupils can define their own curriculum is to miss the details of autonomy within the school day. Even within the constraints of the National Curriculum it is possible for pupils to be independent learners. From reception age, children at Batheaston, as at many other primary schools, learn to choose their own media and materials for the task in hand. They locate the appropriate learning materials within the classroom and school and select and collect them themselves. In this way they develop the skills of independent learners and self-directed resource managers. They take some control over the way in which their time is spent in school. By bringing books and items into school from home to show and share with others, they make their contribution to the direction in which themes and topics are developed. Periodically display areas in the school are designated for the exclusive use of the pupils. This allows them to determine which achievements in which areas are worthy of publicity and acclaim. A paired reading scheme allows older children to assist in the learning of younger ones and as well as enhancing cooperation gives them the opportunity to take some responsibility for the curricular work of the school.

Perhaps the most important formal process with regard to participation in curriculum planning is that which involves the annual questionnaires and parental interviews. Once a year, usually in February, pupils and parents take part in an annual review of how curriculum work is progressing and what the school can do to support it further. This is done through three questionnaires. Parents fill out one of these at home:

Name of Child:

1. Do you think your child is happy at School~   Yes ☐   No☐

2. How would you describe your child: (please tick or cross) Add details if necessary

Confident
Anxious
Cooperative
Able to share
Caring
Able to take turns .
Moody
Cheerful
Tolerant
Thoughtful
Lively
Persevering
Creative
Imaginative
Able to choose own activities
Well-organized
Good at concentrating .
Able to complete activities
Able to listen well.
Able to follow instructions
Good at making decisions
Clearly **understands** parents' expectations for behaviour.
Cooperates with parents' expectations for behaviour.
3. Is there anything that happens at home which might affect your child's performance at school, and that you think we should take into account, e.g. poor sleep pattern; parent shift work demands; parents' separation, etc.
4. Do you think your child mixes happily with other children? In school   ☐   Out of school ☐

---

5. Are there interests, achievements we should record that we might not know about, e.g. cubs, swimming, gym, hobbies, etc?

6. Are there any activities which your child loves or is particularly interested in at school?

7. In school, what do you think your child is really good at, at the moment?

8. What do you think your child needs more help with?

9. What are the most important things you wish your child to develop the next year?

10. Do you think it is best left to the teacher or yourself? Or would you like us to show you ways to help your child with this?

11. If you are able to spend time doing things with your child (e.g. playing, hobbies, outings is this
frequent ☐   regular ☐   occasional ☐
What types of activities do you do?
Do you need ideas? Yes ☐ No ☐

12. We do already ask you to fit in listening to your child reading, sharing books, etc. as part of the PACT scheme. Are you confident to do this?
Would you like some help, e.g. with children who are difficult to motivate?
Yes☐ No☐

13. Did you find the Curriculum/Planning evening helpful? Yes ☐ No ☐ Unable to attend ☐

14. In response to your comments last year, we have acknowledged the need for a similar scheme to support maths activities at home, e.g. sharing simple puzzles and practical activities, once a month. How do you feel about this?

15. We feel that your children will succeed better if they feel that you think that school and learning are important- Please comment.

16. Is there anyone else you feel would have some useful information which would help us in teaching your child e.g., childminder; separated parent; other family member; parent's partner with whom child lives
Please note: Because of the 1991 Childrens Act, we are now required to provide separated parentts with copies of all reports-. Please ensure that we have appropriate details.

17. What do you think are the most important things your children should learn at school to prepare them for the situations they will meet in the future?

18. Apart from making school more stimulating and interesting, do you think having parents in to join the children with their activities has helped your child to learn? Please comment.

19. If you were given support, would you be interested to help at school in any of the following ways?
Around the school generally, e.g. library, bookshop, making equipment, sharing skills with staff or pupils ☐; In your child's class☐; In a different class ☐
Fundraising ☐. Would this be on a regular basis ☐ or occasionally ☐

20. There have been a lot of negative discussions about Education in the media recently. Has this affected your view about our school.

21. Did you feel that the aims identified in the contract last year were easy to fulfil?
For us : ☐ For you: ☐

22. Please use the back of this sheet if there is anything else you would like to tell us about your child, or comment below:

23. Please indicate the time which would be most convenient for you and your partner to meet with your child's teacher for half an hour.
Between 8.45 - 12.00 ☐ 1.00 - 3.00 ☐ 3.00 - 5.00 ☐
Evening meetings could be set up on Tuesday, 1st March, 1994.

Please return this questionnaire by 9th February, 1994. Thank you.
Batheaston Primary 5chool 1991 ©

The teachers complete a parallel questionnaire:

TEACHERS' ASSESSMENT QUESTIONNAIRE

Name of Child

1. Is the child happy at school?   Yes □ No □

Comments:

2. Would you describe the child as:

Confident .
Anxious
Co-operative
Able to share .
Caring
Able to take turns
Moody
Cheerful
Tolerant
Thoughtful
Lively
Persevering
Creative
Imaginative
Able to choose own activities
Well-organized
Good at concentrating
Able to complete activities
Able to listen well
Able to follow instructions
Good at making decisions
Clearly understands teachers' expectations
Co-operates with teacher expectations for behaviour
3. Are there any indications that the child's performance at school is affected by external circumstances, e.g. late arrival, tiredness, enthusiastic parents, etc.
4. Does the child mix happily with other children?   Yes □ No □
5. What evidence do we see of activities at home, e.g. reading
6. What activities do we think the child loves and is particularly interested in?
7. What do we think the child is really good at, at the moment?
8. We think the child needs a little extra help at the moment with:
9. In the next year, the child might need specific help with:
 School: Home:
10. How do you perceive parent interest in helping the child with educational difficulties?
11. Are you happy about the way the PACT scheme is working with this child?

12. Does the child share with you activities done at home?
13. Re: Last year's contract:
14. Does either parent get involved with class activities? Please comment
15. How does the child respond to other adult helpers in school?
16. Any further comments?

Signature   Date

The children fill out a detailed self-assessment form

My name is:
I am [ ] years and [ ] months old in

1. (Please tick)   I enjoy   I'm good at   I'd like help
STORY-
WRITING
HANDWRITING
COMPUTER
SPELLING WORDS
READING
CONSTRUCTION KITS
PAINTING & DRAWING
MATHS ACTIVITIES
SCIENCE
TECHNOLOGY
GEOGRAPHY
P.E.
MAKING MUSIC
SINGING
DANCE
DRAMA
HISTORY
ASSEMBLIES
LISTENING TO STORIES
TALKING TO THE CLASS
WORKING WITH CHILDREN FROM OTHER CLASSES
2. Do you have enough time to finish your work?   YES ☐   NO ☐
If so, which subject is hardest to finish?
3. Do you like the room: Quiet ☐   A bit noisy ☐   Noisy ☐
4. Who is it best for you to sit with to work well? Why?
Do you like it when there are other grown-ups to help you with your work? Yes ☐
No []
5. Where in the room do you like to work best?
6. What is the most Important thing you learn here?
7. What do your parents think is the most important?
8. What are you best at?
9. What would you like to get better at?
10. Do you like being at school? Yes ☐ No ☐ sometimes ☐
11. What do you like about playtimes?
12. What do you NOT like about playtimes?
13. How could we make lunchtimes better?
14. Do you tell your mum or dad about the activities you've been doing Yes ☐ No ☐
15. Are they pleased with you, or do they think you could do better?

16. Do you think you could do better?
17. If you could change something about your class what would it be?
18. Do you find it easy to stay friends with people?
19. Do you think it is important to make your work attractive?   Yes ☐ No ☐
20. Do you llke your work to be displayed on the wall?   Yes ☐ No ☐
21. Do you like your name on it? Yes ☐ No ☐
22. Who do you like to see your work?
23. Do you know where to find everything you need?   Yes ☐ No ☐
24. Do you like to work on your own ☐ In a group ☐ With a partner ☐?
25. Do you have lots of nice work which shows exactly how clever you are, or haven't you shown us yet?
   I have ☐ I haven't ☐
26. What is your favourite thing about school?
   What is your favourite thing to do at home?

|Signature of child: Date:

|Signature of adult: Date:

Batheaston Primary School 1991 ©

The children's contributions show an ability and enthusiasm, even at an early age, to perceive their own progress and their needs. They look at issues such as: the pace at which they work; with whom; in which areas of the curriculum they need help; their friendship skills; their ability to select and organise equipment.

When all three questionnaires have been completed, the parents and the teacher meet to talk about them. At this parent interview, they use the three questionnaires to identify the child's current areas of achievement and ways of developing those further. They also organise together specific support for any difficulties. They concentrate on working out what are the particular skills and activities which need to be the focus for the next year. This is sometimes in terms of subject areas like science, but more frequently it involves a detailed scrutiny of the pupil's development potential: specific targets such as concentration on reading non-fictional books or working on hand-eye coordination in both drawing and writing are then agreed. These targets are then summarised on a Home-School Contract, which entails curricular aims for the child during the following year, both at home and at school:

Name of Child: Class:
Agreed areas of achievement/strengths:

Suggestions for further development: a) At school

b) At home

Areas in which the child could make   Suggestions for
substantial improvement (including   action, both at school and at home
behaviour, in specific terms)

Please use the reverse for special request /other information
Parent(s):
Teacher:
Headteacher:

When the Contract is finalised it is signed by the teacher and the parent and each retains a copy. The Contract is then discussed with the child both at home and at school and the targets remain as a focus for the ensuing year. They are often used as the framework for the more refined individual termly learning targets which again involve the participation of the parents and pupils.

As well as the statutory assessment and reporting required by the National Curriculum, the school has developed profiling (records of achievement) as an appropriate way of monitoring and recording each child's progress. Particular attention is paid to recording both the subject material covered and the level of achievement attained by each child. In this way, profiles are compiled for all the children containing evidence and examples of their learning, copies of reports written for them, teacher-, parent- and self-assessment sheets, specimens of outstanding work, etc. These profiles belong to the children, and access to them is always open: they are sometimes shared together during quiet reading time. They form a cumulative record and history of each child's development in the school. The children take them on to secondary school where they can be continued. The profiles document one way in which the children retain ownership of the curriculum.

Two small final examples may further demonstrate the varieties of this ownership. The school is committed to evaluation of its policies and ensuring that this evaluation is used, where appropriate, to modify practice. The first non-competitive sports day gave rise to considerable discussion among both pupils and parents. It became clear that nearly all the pupils preferred the non-competitive approach but that a number of parents still liked the competitive day. A compromise of having a non-competitive sports day every alternate year was arrived at. A similar conflict occurred over the annual leavers' assembly. The ceremony whereby each leaver came to the front of the hall accompanied by music and then sat facing the audience was recognised as being very emotional. Parents concerned at the tears requested that the leavers should sit facing the front like the other children. This was tried for one year. However, it transpired that the leavers themselves thought the emotion was appropriate to the occasion and so, after a deputation by the pupils to the Year 6 teacher and the headteacher, the original format of the assembly was restored. The ability of the pupils to determine the curriculum in these small but symbolic matters emphasises the school's attempts to give them responsibility for and ownership of their own learning.

Special needs

The ethos of the school is that its learning and behaviour policies will mean that it will be able to educate children perceived to have special needs provided there is adequate support. Special needs are talked about openly, and it is commonly understood that all children might well have such a need at some point of their school career and that therefore many of them will be working on individually designed special tasks. Careful continuous assessment is carried out to try to identify such needs at an early stage. Whenever necessary, additional support is organized, and the general approach is to acknowledge that all children are individual and work at different levels and paces in separate areas of the curriculum.

A special needs teacher works one afternoon each week to support the work of the coordinator. As part of this time, the special needs teacher plans appropriate activities in conjunction with the class teacher and provides guidance and training for the teaching assistants. Every day all the teaching assistants devote from half to one hour of individual support for children with special needs. Class teachers use the specific information about a child with special needs to inform their daily plans and accordingly to differentiate learning activities. When events and outings are planned it is acknowledged by the whole group from the outset that these will present a challenge to the behaviour of some pupils. Part of the preparation then is to make suggestions as to activities that children can do on a bus journey or who they should sit next to, how to handle meetings with new children or adults, ideas for groupings, etc. In this way any children with potential behaviour difficulties are motivated not to disappoint the support and commitment of the group.

A final example may illustrate the general awareness and sympathy for particular educational needs. The footballers wanted a new set of school kit and decided to raise the money themselves. The whole of the class discussed what would be the most effective sponsorship approach to parents. When they settled on the idea of a - subsequently popular - sponsored spell, the difficulties of two children within the group were recognised. The children developed the solution of having highly differentiated spelling lists. The awareness of differential achievement was handled openly but respectfully and a joint solution was found for a commonly owned difficulty.

This chapter has focused on policy and practice in a particular primary school. These policies are not at all in themselves unique. Many other schools are pursuing at least equally progressive policies with regard to children's involvement and special educational needs. Rather the example has allowed us to focus on the way in which a school attempts to walk the tightrope between the need for social control and conformity and the development of the full potential of each individual. This balance operates between the fearful polar opposites of our society: repression and growth, indoctrination and education, conformity and individuality, totalitarianism and democracy. Between these appalling alternatives every teacher and every headteacher must walk. Policies which seek to ensure the involvement and participation of young children in their primary schools are a way of ensuring that, when we fall, it is in a particular direction.

Chapter 2.4

PARENTS AND SCHOOLS: DEVELOPING A PARTNERSHIP APPROACH TO ADVOCACY

Sarah Sandow

The interface between home and school is crucial for extending the positive involvement of children with SEN in the life of the whole school. It is also an area of activity which is fraught with tensions and difficulties. Traditionally schools in Britain have not welcomed parental participation. Parents themselves have been diffident about 'interfering' with what goes on in school, and even today are reluctant to be thought to be 'difficult' by their children's teachers. However, things are changing, and this chapter reviews some of the reasons for this, with particular reference to recent legislation, and goes on to suggest strategies for enabling more effective liaison between home and school.

The first question we should ask is: *should* parents be advocates for their children? The question appears to admit only a positive reply, but before we accept it uncritically, it should be remembered that the interests of parents and children are not necessarily the same. The many sad cases of neglect and abuse, and the even more numerous examples known to all of us of parents who have forced children into unsuitable career or social choices against their better judgement, mean that we must be cautious at least of assuming that parents' and children's views and interests are always compatible. Nevertheless, it would be ridiculous to suggest that parents are never able to make dispassionate and realistic judgements, or that their views should be disregarded.

During a child's educational career, he or she is the focus of concern for the authorities at several levels: national, local and school. Nationally, especially since the present government has rejected the arms-length relationship characteristic of earlier times, parents have been subject to a number of assumptions about their interests and priorities, expressed in a range of official communications. Locally, the education authorities have had to match their concern for parental views with the responsibility laid on them to provide, until the introduction of grant-maintained status for some schools, for all the children in a locality, at a time of diminishing resources. At school level, parents have been offered a series of more or less benign relationships, and teachers have had to deal with individual parents within the framework constructed by the school. A relatively small subset of these parents have children with special educational needs. Some of these parents may have had long, certainly anxious and perhaps contentious relationships with providers in schools, clinics and hospitals. They will have become accustomed to fighting for services for their children and may appear initially as suspicious and belligerent. Others, whose children's difficulties have been more recently identified, may still be in a state of what was long ago called 'novelty shock' (Wolfensberger and Menolascino 1970). Their relationships with schools and with LEAs may also be problematic.

Parents and government: the consumer-advocate

During the last fifteen years the approach of government to parents of children at school has changed dramatically, Although, as pointed out by Walford (1994), some parents always exercised choice among different forms of educational provision, the vast majority confined that choice to denominational or non-denominational schools wherever they happened to live. Since 1979 however, the government has promoted choice of provision as a new ethic, with the implied corollary that choice is, in fact, available to all. In fact, although even in the 1980 Education Act preference was available, actual choice has been confined to a few. Gradually, throughout the 1980s, government documents moved from promoting parental interest and influence in the way schools were run to a much more imperious interpretation of the relationship between parents and schools; while ostensibly promoting 'partnership', government was actually substituting the concept of parent power, which it expected would cause schools to become more formal, traditional places, incompatible with the 'trendy' teaching methods of which they so heartily disapproved. Thus, while the White Paper *Better Schools* (DES, 1985) promoted the idea of a Record of Achievement (ROA) for all pupils which could provide evidence of a wide range of achievements and interests, later in the decade ministerial enthusiasm was tempered, and while the ROA remains, it is seen as very inferior to formal examination results. There are no exhortations for parents to compare the effectiveness of different schools' preparation of the ROA; on the other hand parents *are* expected to compare academic performances, and to be able to make informed judgements between them.

The underlying assumptions about the basis for parent choice are visible from the Parents' Charter (DES, 1991; DfE, 1994d) which stipulates certain characteristics of a school's prospectus. This is required to describe the school's achievement, in terms of examinations passed and attendance rates; the arrangements for sex education (and how to withdraw children from this), religious observance, careers education and work experience. The rules for deciding who has a right to a place in the school must be explained in the prospectus, and every secondary school must say how many parents applied, and how many children got places. Thus parents are assumed to be obsessed with outcomes, suspicious of sex education, approving of religious observance, and highly competitive. Popular schools will be good schools (for all children, whatever their individual characteristics) and can be judged by the length of the queue outside. While the right to withdraw from sex education and religious assembly is stressed, there is no identified right to withdraw a child from testing. There is a right to influence the way the school is run, first by attending the annual parents meeting (the Charter appears to assume that this was a new development), next, to stand for election as a parent governor (ditto), and finally to 'force' a ballot and to vote on grant-maintained status. This in itself implies resistance on the part of vested interests to an obvious change for the better.

This picture of the 'parent as customer' shopping around for certain school characteristics is challenged by Knight (1992), and by Walford (1994), who cites a range of studies which demonstrate that parental choice is influenced by a much wider range of characteristics than suggested above, including pastoral care, travelling safety and convenience, and not least, children's preferences. In one study quoted, 60% of secondary age children claimed to have made the choice of school themselves, and a further 30% that it was a joint decision with their parents. Thus it may be said that many, if not all, parents act as joint advocates with their children, and that their advocacy relates as much to happiness as to achievement. Anecdotal evidence supports this view. The *Independent* (24.11.94) cites a range of parents interviewed who sought happiness rather than academic performance:

> I don't think the league tables made a hoot of difference. We judged the schools for ourselves, and the decision wasn't to do with exam results. Other things were far more important. We wanted some involvement with the school and for Dorothy to have a social life, so we weren't looking too far afield. We looked at quality of teaching and care of the child, whether pupils felt comfortable, safe and valued; these were the factors that weighed heavily with us. We wanted her to be in a school that would make the best of her.

Nevertheless, *Choice and Diversity* (DES 1992) pursued the now received view (in government circles) that parents were interested in power and control, and indeed, knew 'best the needs of their children - certainly better than educational theorists or administrators, better even than our mostly excellent teachers'. The barely hidden sneer about the competence of professionals suggests that what is called partnership is actually dictatorship, hardly conducive to creating good working relationships between parents and schools. It appears that successive Ministers of Education have encouraged the development of the parent advocate as a demanding consumer rather than a participant in the educational process.

A clearly identified system of 'What to do if things go wrong' was included in the updated Parent's Charter (DfE, *op. cit.*). This outlined a series of actions which parents could take, from speaking to the teacher or head teacher, appealing to the governing body, or to the local council, and finally to the Secretary of State. The Charter also described an 'independent appeal procedures which means that you can often have your side of the case looked at by a separate committee or tribunal' and pointed out that committees which look at decisions on school places and expulsions from school must now include an 'independent' member as well as people chosen by the local council or a member of the school's governing body.

Government views about parents in general have been echoed in the treatment of *some* parents of children with special educational needs. The 1981 Act, even though it was but a shadow of what was intended by the Warnock Committee, did promote partnership, and in the statementing procedure, encouraged parent advocacy. In the numerous schemes for pre-school home intervention, parents played an increasing part in developing children's skills and this extended to participation in the early years of special schooling. The 1988 Education Reform Act, however, with a philosophy of seeking excellence rather than responding to need, had little to say to parents of children with SEN. Indeed the emphasis on disapplication of the National Curriculum for some children suggested disenfranchisement rather than an opportunity for promoting the interests of parents and children with SEN. The intended publication of league tables increased the pressures, and the eventual dissemination of GCSE examination pass lists for all children in the relevant age bracket, including those at special schools, further confirmed the second-class status of pupils with SEN. During the late 1980s an increased number of exclusions and a reduction in residential and other special school places reduced the choices open to parents and children. However, the 1993 Education Act redressed the balance somewhat by formally promoting partnership between schools and parents.

However the framework of appeals and complaint systems reinforces the view that parents and educators are naturally opposed. A parent can appeal if a place is not offered at the school of choice. If not satisfied with the way the appeal was conducted into allocation or exclusion, a complaint can be made to the Local Government Ombudsman. Parents can also appeal if the National Curriculum is disapplied against their wishes. In the case of exclusion, parents have the right to have full information, to put a case to the governing body, and to appeal to the special committee.

By contrast with the academically driven, confrontational approach promoted for the majority, the 1993 Education Act and its associated Code of Practice (COP) appear to suggest a different kind of relationship for the parents of childrem with SEN. The success of the COP is still to be evaluated. A good deal will depend on the ability of schools to engage with parents in a partnership which may be at odds with the purchaser-provider model espoused by the DfE.

Altogether, therefore, it appears that government has pursued two different approaches to parent advocacy: on the one hand, it mandates parents to confront schools and LEAs, saying explicitly (in *Choice and Diversity*) that parents know best what their children need; on the other it promotes partnership and collaboration between parent and school, especially where learning difficulties are concerned.

Parents and LEAs: the lost link

It is hard to separate parental relationships with LEAs from the influence of national government. Local Management of Schools and the misleading statements about parental choice (really parental preference) have removed much of the influence of the LEA with parents and children. The reduction of budgets to a bare minimum for support services including those for special needs, educational psychology and education welfare, means that parents would be forgiven for thinking that LEAs had little interest in or concern for their children.

As far as children with identified special needs are concerned, probably the most important contact is that related to the process of making a statement. Again straitened resources and some inefficiencies (Audit Commission, 1992) have meant that the time taken to make a statement has become very long, sometimes up to three years, and even in the most efficient LEAs it rarely met the six month target. In addition, some of the services needed, such as physiotherapy or speech therapy, are not provided by the LEA but must be bought in from the equally under-resourced AHAs.

In these circumstances it is not surprising that parents have been less happy with the specialist services provided by the LEA, relative to those made available by schools and individual teachers (Sandow, *et al*. 1986).

There are some positive links, however. LEAs have been quick to apply for and use central funds through Education Support Grants, for computer education, early intervention programmes such as the Portage Project, school attendance, and currently, parent-support systems.

Home and school: who communicates with whom?

In 1986, the National Consumer Council argued that existing formal channels of communication between parents and schools were often an ineffective way of consulting and disseminating information. They recommended that initial teacher training should include specific training in dealing with parents and pupils; that HMI should assess a school's ability to involve and consult parents. In 1994, they found in a second report on home-school relations, that few schools achieved a genuine partnership. They cited a Consumers' Association survey which found that four out of five schools failed to produce all the legally required information in prospectuses (Bastiani and Doyle, 1994).

Despite strenuous efforts it appears that some schools still find it difficult to achieve a reasonable tone when giving information. The following are real examples of 'standard letters' sent to parents from one school:

> Dear Parent,
> During the recent termly review of pupil progress your son/daughter was identified by teaching staff as giving cause for concern in a number of subject areas.
> I am writing to ask you to make an appointment to come in to school so that we can discuss ways to improve the situation.
> I feel sure that you will wish to work with us to help your child so that difficulties can be overcome at an early stage.
> Yours sincerely

> Dear Parent,
> I regret to inform you that we are dissatisfied with some of the homework   is producing. Full details of our concern can be found in his/her journal. It is our experience that regular homework establishes good study habits and is essential in many subjects to re-inforce the work which is done in school.
> When school and home co-operate to ensure that homework is completed satisfactorily, pupils undoubtedly benefit. I am therefore writing to ask you to assist us in monitoring your child's homework carefully for the next four weeks in the hope that between us we can effect and sustain the necessary improvement.
> Please use your child's journal to acknowledge receipt of this letter.
> Yours sincerely

Bastiani (1987) identified four ideologies of relationship between parents and schools: Compensation, Communication, Accountability and Participation. Compensatory education, born out of the determination to do something about perceived inner-city deprivation and its educational effects was, despite highminded efforts which found their fullest expression in the Plowden Report, essentially incompatible with a positive relationship between parents and schools, and reinforced the social class divide between working-class homes and middle-class schools. Naturally, nowadays most schools are unwilling to admit any element of compensation in their relationship with parents.

Communication, in Bastiani's model, is more problematic than at first it seems. For schools are the leaders in this relationship; schools identify what information shall be transmitted to parents, and in turn parents react and respond receptively, using the channels of communication which are opened to them. In turn, these channels are provided by the schools. Such a system depends on the acceptance by parents of school systems, school mores, and school definitions of appropriate communication. While this may sometimes be a comfortable relationship, it may not always be a productive one, for the parents may accede to a view of their children and their children's potential which may not be particularly positive, and to a form of education which may not be the most appropriate for them. Perhaps the two letters quoted above are rather unfortunate examples of this form of 'communication'. However, they are not alone: reviewing a sample of 125 prospectuses from secondary schools suggests information-giving rather than partnership:

> 'Parents are *informed* of discipline problems' (my italics)

Others give details of the Governing body and ask for parental involvement in school functions. One prospectus stated (after 15 pages): 'The most important communication with parents is the report'. Communication in others is seen as mainly one way: with a rather discouraging 'we hope parents will feel sufficient confidence in the school to approach Form Tutors, Year Heads or Heads of School whenever concerns about children arise'.

There are exhortations to check that homework is done, not let children out until it is finished, check the homework diary, etc., etc. Sometimes it seems that parents are enlisted as policemen, e.g.:

> 'The Parent's aims'
> (or duties ?)
> - To support the pupil's learning
> - To show interest in school work and progress
> - To ensure pupils have basic school equipment
> - To ensure homework is completed
> - To attend parents' evenings
> - To support school uniform'
> - To ensure punctuality and regular attendance

Communication here is definitely designed to secure compliance, and parents could be forgiven for being somewhat overawed by it. In other cases, it appears that prospectuses try to represent partnership as their preferred model, but are overpowered by the legal requirement to adopt an accountability model. We would suggest that the partnership (participation) and purchaser-provider (accountability) relationships are incompatible. In a partnership, roles are complementary: in the purchaser/provider relationship the roles are confrontational. Purchasers may demand, but providers set rules: 'caveat emptor' is the rule here as well as in the department store, and above all, 'the management reserves the right to refuse admission' to those who do not keep the rules. However, not all schools present so defensive a front, even on the completion of homework:

> Sometimes children can reach the point where they worry so much they are unable to proceed with the work. If you sense that a piece of homework is causing this sort of distress or concern, you may want to tell the subject teacher by writing a brief note on your child's exercise book and then advising your child to move on to another piece of work.

Exceptionally, one prospectus included a very 'user friendly' statement, which is worth quoting at length:

> Parents know their children better than we do at school; we know children in mass better than many parents. Between us, we can solve most problems We shall try to uphold the values which parents want and we hope that parents, in turn, will support the school. If something is said or done which undermines what you are trying to do, please let us know, and talk about it.
>
> The partnership in bringing up young people generally works well, but there are some standard problems:
>
> 1. Children quite often play off home against school or the other way round. Be prepared for that to happen, and contact us at school to check if you are worried.
>
> 2. We try to make sensible demands of children and of home. If it seems that we are not doing (so), telephone. We all have a home life.
>
> 3. Sometimes the rules aimed at controlling a large school seem unreasonable - as if we don't trust your son or daughter. Please try to support us, remembering that children in the mass behave differently from when they are on their own.
>
> 4. Finally it must be remembered that we can't please all of the people all of the time. We'll try to meet your individual wishes

but you will need to bear with us at other times because a majority of parents may think differently from you.

What can parents do for their children?

Parents help their children by providing a quiet working base and taking an interest in both what they have done at school each day and in their homework. The chance to explore future careers by meeting people in other walks of life is valuable.

Children also benefit from books, magazines or any experiences which will broaden their horizons. Teachers will help with recommendations, but having books at home is a great help, as is making sure that young people join and use local libraries, or the van schemes.

Visits to local places of interest, museums or historic buildings in other towns, or travel of all kinds, also give a wider view of the world.

There is nothing better than family time spent together. During the years a child is at secondary school, he or she begins to establish a separate way of life, often through friendships. Parents feel that children need less attention, and so begin to pick up the threads of their lives again. However, our experience is that young people need to know their parents care, and need their support and interest longer than is sometimes thought. Family outings, visits and meals at home together are always worthwhile.

Another school included a comment inviting advocacy:

Each child is issued with a "Log Book and Personal Record of Achievement". It helps all of us monitor homework and students' day to day organisation. Parents and tutors are invited to comment on a daily or weekly basis. Equally, if you are proud of your child's achievements and feel that we ought to know, please contact your child's tutor. It is an important part of the School's ethos to celebrate achievement.

These extracts echo Bastiani and Doyle's (1994) version of partnership, which states that:

an effective school is characterised by, among other things, an active commitment to improving the quality of its work with parents. More specifically, this means

- developing more effective means of communicating about the life and work of the school in ways appropriate to its parents;
- providing a range of opportunities for parents to become actively involved in their children's schooling;
- a recognition of the role of parents as educators themselves and a practical ability to capitalise on their influence; generating the sense of a common enterprise, based upon shared responsibility and joint action.   (Bastiani and Doyle, 1994, p. 21).

They sound more like partnership than the limited version promoted in the 1994 Parents' Charter, where 'making sure (the child) goes to school regularly, and on time...supporting the school's policy on homework and behaviour' are the main things emphasised. However, it may be questioned how much of this is reaching parents in any case.

The advent of Grant Maintained Schools (GMS) and City Technology Colleges (CTCs) and the starving of LEA budgets have led to uneven resourcing, and as a consequence, schools have become more dependent upon parents as financial supporters. This means that fundraising is the most visible form of parent involvement in school. Certainly, the Parent Teacher Association is billed in most Prospectuses as the most obvious and welcome form of parent support. This must encourage parents to feel that the only acceptable form of participation is donation, which in turn disenfranchises those who are unable to be contributors.

League tables include data on attendance as well as on examination results. 'Good' schools are those which have devised ways of ensuring high attendance. Attendance can become a bone of contention where there is condoned absence or where parents cannot control children. Placing pressure on parents may increase attendance rates, but is this compatible with partnership?

Schools often complain about that significant core of parents whom they do not reach, but these may well be those who are hesitant or resistant to the 'cheese and wine' view of collaboration. It is now increasingly recognised that relatively few children, at any rate in towns and cities, grow up in traditional nuclear families and even these often need both parents to be earning, often in jobs with unsocial hours. So schools need to design new ways of working with parents, and also to attempt to engage parents *with* their children in school-based activities. The Community Education movement attempted this in the 1960s and 1970s, and however unfashionable now, it did generate the kind of relationship which recognised and respected the worlds which children and their families inhabited (Sandow and Garner, 1994).

The traditional form of parents' evening carries with it not only certain formal kinds of encounter between teachers and parents, but it also epitomises a system in which children are not consulted about their own education. Such a tradition ascribes to them a role as the property of their parents. The 1989 Children Act reminds us that children have a right to a voice in their own affairs, and this is reinforced to some extent in the Special Educational Needs COP following the 1993 Education Act, of which more later. Bastiani and Doyle say it is time to reintroduce formal pupil participation in school affairs, via membership of governing bodies (abolished in 1986). There is no reason why parents *and* children should not participate in decision making.

Parents and children with special educational needs

Parents of children with special needs have been in the forefront of movements for parental advocacy. The 1981 Act responded to the emphasis in the Warnock Report on parental participation, an emphasis itself derived from the passionate endorsement of the concept by a wide range of groups which gave evidence to it. In addition, special schools had already begun to accept parent participation in the classroom, and to encourage parents to undertake a teaching role. Parents of children with severe learning difficulties had been joining in or even leading their children's education fo a number of years. There were some problems with this as well as many advantages. Parents engaged in early intervention programmes were often cast in the role of student, or assistant to the expert (Sandow *et al.* 1986) and the transition from home teaching to school was not always happy and successful. The new relationship, and the consequent diminution of parent power and influence, was and is not always easy to cope with.

Similarly there may also be problems in mainstream schools, especially at secondary level because there is no national experience of parental involvement at this stage. In particular, there is no tradition of collective action as in the USA or parts of mainland Europe. Apart from the obvious fundraising tasks, relations here have involved individual parents and individual schools. Organisations such as the National Council of Parent Teacher Associations (NCPTA), the Campaign for State Education and the Advisory Centre for Education are often seen as antagonistic to government and therefore potentially dangerous. Other groups such as MENCAP or the Spastics Society (now renamed SCOPE), while having a role in special schools, are more likely to be seen as recipients of charity collections.

The parents' version of the COP DfE 1994b) states explicitly 'You are an active partner with your child's school' and further 'If your child is having difficulties the school *may ask him or her about what help he or she would like* (my italics). Children can be very worried if they are having problems at school. Your child will need your support and encouragement so that you and your child can work closely with the school.' It is notable that there is no equivalent statement in the Parent's Charter where the emphasis is on disagreement, dissatisfaction and complaint. Once again, it seems, parents of children with special needs are in the vanguard.

The COP itself provides the most complete and explicit requirements for parental participation ever included in a formal document. It is worth looking in detail at the four paragraphs which consider relationships with parents.

> The relationship between parents of children with special educational needs and the school which their child is attending has a crucial bearing on the child's educational progress and the effectiveness of any school based action. Most schools already have effective working relationships with parents including the parents of children with special educational needs. School based arrangements should ensure that assessment reflects a sound and comprehensive knowledge of a child and his or her responses to a variety of carefully planned and recorded actions which take account of the wishes, feelings and knowledge of parents at all stages. Children's progress will be diminished if their parents are not seen as partners in the educational process with unique knowledge and information to impart. Professional help can seldom be wholly effective unless it builds upon parents' capacity to be involved and unless parents consider that professionals take account of what they say and treat their views and anxieties as intrinsically important. (DfE, 1994a, 2.28)

It is notable that the importance of this relationship is recognised specifically for children with SEN. All children benefit from such a positive association. However, in view of the extracts included above, it is questionable whether this is in fact the case. If the wishes, feelings and knowledge of parents of children without special needs are not correctly identified as has been suggested above, how sure are we that those of these parents are understood? Or is it that wishes for happiness, security and locality are more comprehensible when emanating from these parents, and therefore more allowable?

> The school-based stages should therefore utilise parents' own distinctive knowledge and skills and contribute to parents' own understanding of how best to help their child. The identification of a special educational need may be alarming to parents. In some instances parents may consider that their early concerns were given insufficient attention. Schools should not inte.pret a failure to participate as indicating a lack of interest or willingness.Parents may feel they are being blamed for their child's difficulties when the school first raises questions with them. Nonetheless, schools should make every effort to encourage parents to recognise that they have responsibilities towards their child, and that the most effective provision will be made when they are open and confident in working in partnership with the school and with professionals. (DfE, 1994a, 2.29)

The COP is directed to teachers who are considering children who may, eventually, be the subject of a statement. However, there are many other children who form perhaps a significant number of the 'twenty percent who may at some time have special educational needs' (DES, 1978). It does sometimes seem that there is an unacknowledged division between parents of children with unexpected intellectual difficulties, who are given every kind of support, and the much larger group of disadvantaged families whose lack of participation is put down to fecklessness and personal preoccupation. Among their children may be those who are seen as disruptive by teachers, who may be less inclined to 'utilise parents' own distinctive knowledge and skills', especially if they feel that these parents are the source of the problem. The way that cooperation is sought, as has been seen from the prospectus extracts above, can vary from a hectoring demand for cooperation to an understanding and lengthy discursion which recognises the dilemmas of both parents and children.

> If the child has a behavioural difficulty or is following a developmental activity of any kind which requires a structured approach in school, reinforcement at home by parents will be crucial. Many parents can become discouraged by their child's continuing difficulties at home and at school, and feel themselves to be inadequate in dealing with the difficulty. The governing body, head teacher and the SEN coordinator should consider how the school can support such parents. (DfE, 1994a, 2.30)

Such programmes have traditionally operated in the early years of education. It is true that the most common cause of failure is ineffective communication and lack of generalisation of learned skills. As time goes by, parents need more support in maintaining a management programme in the face of early setbacks. Too often programmes are set up and not monitored or modified when they falter.

> Some parents may have problems in understanding written information and communicating with schools because of literacy difficulties or if English or Welsh is not their first language. The school should consider how best to involve such parents, and whether to make written information available in the main languages of the local community, using the resources of relevant community-based organisations. In some instances taped or videotaped information packs may be helpful, particularly in illustrating the type of provision and support which is available, and how parents may help their children at home. (DfE, 1994a, 2.31)

There was no sustained evidence in the prospectuses studied, that schools were ready to take on the responsibility of communicating in languages other than English. It may be, of course that such documentation was available, but was not sent in response to the general request for information.

> Schools should be aware of the definitions of 'parent' and 'parental responsibility', which are in the Glossary. They should know in each instance who should be regarded as a parent of a particular child and who should therefore be consulted regarding the child's progress in school. It is often the case that adults in more than one household qualify as parents for the purposes of the Education Acts. All those with parental responsibility for a child have.rights and responsibilities towards the child: a school should endeavour to keep records of all those with parental responsibility and involve them as much as possible in the child's education. However, this will not always be practical and a school may be able to discharge its responsibilities by dealing with the parent who has day-to-day care of the child. .Where parents disagree among themselves about decisions regarding their child's education, they can apply to the Court for resolution under the Children Act 1989 (DfE, 1994a, 2.32)

This paragraph reveals a developing perception that traditional nuclear families are no longer typical of those with children at school today. It suggests recognition of the social realities which Bastiani and Doyle (1994) say is still lacking in much work with parents that currently takes place. The more one reads the COP the more astonishing it is that these positive statements and careful reviews of practice are confined to special educational needs!

Parents are expected to be consulted in the construction of Individual Education Plans (IEPs) at Stage 2 of the identification process. At Stage 3 they are invited to review meetings. They are encouraged, in the parent's version of the Code, to be involved at all stages. to manage meetings by writing down worries, or by taking a friend, relative or 'named person' with them. Views are actively invited and information given about procedures and time limits. Asking the child's own views is mentioned *five times* in this short document. (It is not mentioned once in the updated 'Parent's Charter' [DfE, 1994e]). It is as yet too soon to assess the value of this complex system, or to examine the characteristics of those who make use of it. The booklet *Special Educational Needs Tribunals: How to appeal* (DfE, 1994c) explains the procedures of the new Tribunals, and is similarly well written, unambiguous and answers all questions clearly.

At the time of writing, we wait to see whether Tribunals will operate smoothly, and if parents from all sections of the community will feel able to use them. One group who certainly will do so are the parents of children identified as having specific learning difficulties or 'dyslexia'. Riddell *et al.* (1994) have explored relationship between these (mainly middle-class) parents and schools or LEAs. They found that whereas 'the notion of individual rights (has the) potential to secure a greater share of the education budget for children with SEN', it is only utilised by a very small number, and in opposition to school policies, methods and priorities. Integration, in-class support and an holistic approach, Riddell found, were resisted by parents of children with 'dyslexia' in favour of a medical model, withdrawal and one-to-one teaching. Riddell drew attention to the characteristics of this group as critical consumers, whose views were not so easily dismissed as those of ordinary working-class parents.

Parents of dyslexic children, it is argued, have taken on a consumer role and adopted a confrontational stand, seeing providers as enemies. In seeking extra provision for their own children, they promote an intrinsic medical model for their children's difficulties, resist the idea of the continuum, and reject environmental or curricular modification in favour of withdrawal from the classroom and one-to-one teaching. They therefore successfully subvert the system by redirecting SEN budget away from most children. In doing so, they are being 'consumer parents' as the government wishes, but at the expense of the rest.

It may be argued that they are also presenting a successful model to other parents, who already feel more comfortble with a medical explanation and often shop around for diagnoses, finding it hard to accept the professional view that it is more important to identify a teaching and learning programme than to fix a label on a child's difficulty (Hellier, 1994). If the COP and its clearly identified stages can redirect parental energies in this way it will be very valuable. Otherwise this consumer model will disenfranchise and disadvantage many more children than it advantages. If all parents were undertaking such a consumer role the result could well be confrontation rather than collaboration.

Conclusion: pointers for good practice

Despite all the problems which will undoubtedly surface about the operation of the COP in schools, that section which deals with parental involvement gives a positive framework within which relations between home and school can develop. Schools need to look carefully at their recruitment literature to make sure it reflects joint action for children and not merely demands for acquiesence in policies currently perceived as desirable. In addition, they need to find ways of involving parents as a whole group, other than by inviting them to make financial contributions. Certainly, as long as parents' influence at school, and their role as advocates, is confined to their own children, there is little prospect of a genuine partnership developing. Indeed Hegarty (1993) questions whether in such circumstances partnership is a useful concept, although he accepts that some activities may express a degree of mutuality. However he does not include in a discussion of such processes any consideration of joint action by parents. As we have noted, government is distrustful of group action taken and views expressed by, for example, the NCPTA (they were dismissed as 'neanderthal' by the former Secretary of State for Education). However, this organisation has more than 8,000 branches in England and Wales and can lift group activity beyond the mere raising of money. Advocacy by parents must move beyond particular loyalties. 'Part of the vision of a world which is more than just a market place regulated by heirarchies is one in which people stand together, act from a sense of their common lot and their common good' (Tyne, 1994).

Chapter 2.5

SUPPORTING ADVOCACY AND SELF-ADVOCACY: THE ROLE OF THE ALLIED PROFESSIONS

Irvine S. Gersch and Barbara Gersch

This chapter first outlines some practical advocacy and self-advocacy projects undertaken, including a pupil-involvement project initiated within an educational psychology service, resulting in a student self-report as part of the assessment process.

Secondly, a number of different professionals who play a key role in the process of identifying and assessing SEN, were interviewed about their current practice in listening to and involving children in their assessments, and acting as advocates.

The Chapter concludes with a discussion of some professional problems and constraints to advocacy and self-advocacy, before suggesting some implications for the future practice of teachers and other professionals working in this field.

The concept of advocacy and self-advocacy in education

During the past ten years, there has been a clear national, and to some extent international, trend towards what is variously called empowerment and democratisation, consumerism, customer care, and giving people choices over decisions. The UN Convention and other legal developments have aimed to extend human rights, and the human rights movement has gathered support throughout the world, at governmental, management and individual levels. Not surprisingly, the picture is not a simple one; there are many examples of abuses of human rights, opposition to such developments, legal changes which are restrictive, and negative practices and events.

In the UK, the fields of education and SEN have not been shaded from such developments, and there has been some movement, albeit patchy and perhaps more limited than some would wish, to involve children and young people more actively in decisions made about them, in their assessments and in their school life.

It is our contention that whilst more can be done to increase the participation of children in decisions made about them, such factors as recent legislation, teacher support, public attitudes, the success of pupil involvement schemes and the growing experience and expectation of children and parents are all factors encouraging and stimulating the further progress of this trend toward increasing the involvement of children and young people.

Advocacy has two main elements in relation to the work of professionals in the area of SEN. For a professional to be an advocate, he or she must be able to support or defend the child, and a logical prerequisite is that the professional should be clear about what aspect of the child's case they are pleading for, supporting or defending. In our experience, the relationship between the professional and the child can be complicated, interacting in subtle and diffuse ways with other significant players, such as parents, teachers and the professional's own employers and colleagues.

Further, the child's 'case' is often far from clear or singular. Indeed, in real life, a child's ideas, preferences and attitudes can change dramatically over short periods of time, under certain circumstances and if exposed to certain events and challenges. Attitudes and preferences are not always expressed in a one-off, clear-cut way, but represent points on a journey of thinking, examining, sorting, analysing and then deciding, and perhaps reconsidering preferences, over a period of time.

Within education, schools and SEN there are a number of areas on which child advocacy and self-advocacy might impinge. These include decision making about the school generally, the assessment of the child's strengths and weaknesses, SEN, individual educational plans, SEN provision and arrangements needed, and choice of school the child wishes to attend. Professionals could be involved in playing an advocacy role in any of the above aspects of the child's school life.

The level to which children themselves will be able to advocate their own views and ideas, within each of the above elements, will depend upon:

(a) the ethos of the school,
(b) the attitudes of teachers, headteachers and governors,
(c) the maturity, skills and ability of the child,
(d) the attitude of the child's parents,

(e) the attitude and propensity of other professionals,
   and perhaps
(f) the attitude, maturity and culture of the children in the
   school.

Naturally, in real life, there is a complex interaction between all these factors, which may be difficult to distinguish and disentangle.

In reality, teachers and allied professionals are simply not pure advocates; indeed it is interesting to compare their roles with those of barristers, who do take on a pure and untarnished advocacy and self-advocacy role within the English legal system. Currently, barristers in private practice are totally independent, they cannot be employed, they have a code of ethics which requires them to defend their client without any personal bias, it is absolutely clear who their client is, they receive rigorous training in advocacy and self-advocacy, negotiation and legal skills, and they may not act for a client if they have any conflict of interest. Teachers and allied professionals, in contrast, who wish to adopt an advocacy role, are working within a non-purist environment. They may come into direct conflict with their employers, their brief is often unclear, they probably have little training in negotiation and advocacy, and there may be other considerations which they have to balance. In short, there is a limit to the extent to which they can act as true child advocates.

This could lead workers in this field to wonder whether going down the road of pupil self-advocacy might have much to commend it. If we could train and encourage children to express their own views, ideas and preferences, and to represent their wishes in a polite, assertive yet clear way, we might actually be doing more of a service to our children in the long term. Such a stance would not rule out the notion of having advocates to represent children, but would entail us always involving the child actively, and directly, in the process.

Finally, it is worth commenting upon the concept of pupil involvement, to which we will return in the third part of this chapter. It has been argued by the author (Gersch,I., 1987;1992) that it might be helpful to consider the degree of pupil involvement at any one time, or for any particular purpose, as lying along a hypothetical continuum from 'minimal involvement' to a 'high degree of involvement', as depicted in figure 1 below. The issue is about increasing active pupil participation incrementally, rather than regarding pupil involvement as an 'all or one' concept.

0 1 2	3 4 5	6 7 8	9 10
Minimal pupil involvement	Moderate pupil involvement	Reasonably active pupil involvement	High degree of pupil involvement

Figure 1   A Continuum of pupil involvement
Source : Chapter 2, p.34 in T. Cline (1992) *The Assessment of Special Educational Needs: international perspectives*, Croom Helm.
and Chapter 10, p.167 in T. Bowers (1987) *SEN and Human Resource Management*, Routledge. (Reprinted with kind permission of the publishers.

Recent Legislative Developments

Several critical pieces of recent legislation, both internationally and within the UK, have gone a considerable way in ensuring that the views of children are taken seriously. At an international level, the United Nations Convention on the Rights of the Child, adopted by the UN in 1989, and ratified by the UK government in 1991, includes several critical articles relevant to child advocacy and self-advocacy. As of August 1994, the convention has been adopted by 175 countries. Article 3 states that 'In all actions, whether undertaken by public or private social welfare institutions, courts of law, administrative authorities or legislative bodies, the best interests of the child shall be a primary consideration.' Article 12 indicates that all states signing the convention

> ...shall assure to the child who is capable of forming his or her own views the right to express those views freely in all matters affecting the child, the views of the child being given due weight in accordance with the age and maturity of the child.

With regard to children with SEN, Article 23 makes it clear that

> ...a mentally or physically disabled child should enjoy a full and decent life, in conditions which ensure dignity, promote self reliance and facilitate the child's active participation in the community.

The 1989 Children Act has established that the child's welfare should be paramount in deciding all questions about the child's upbringing, and further that due consideration must be given to the ascertainable wishes and feelings of the child, bearing in mind his or her age and understanding.

There is no doubt that children do now attend court more frequently than in the past, following changes brought about by the 1991 Criminal Justice Act and that courts have attempted to adapt to enable children to contribute as comfortably as possible. The use of video technology, screens and preparatory materials for children have all been developed in recent years. The first author, for example, was asked to advise one court about the impact of furniture upon children's behaviour and make suggestions about waiting areas for young children.

Children with learning difficulties have also won the right to sue an LEA for failing to meet their special needs, even after they had left school (Court of Appeal, April 1994). The 1993 Education Act, although not containing a direct reference to pupil involvement, provides the primary legislation for the publication of the Code of Practice for the Identification and Assessment of SEN.

Pages 14 and 15 of the Code reiterate earlier guidance that schools should make every effort to identify the ascertainable views and wishes of the child or young person about his or her current and future education, detailing the benefits of involving children in assessments, and giving examples of actions schools might take.

Since, in the production of this policy, all professionals and schools will need to have due regard to the Code of Practice, and the policy must provide information about assessment arrangements, provision and evaluation, it appears implicit that ways of involving pupils throughout will need to be considered and included in the school's SEN final policy document. Governing bodies have a statutory duty to publish information about, and report on, the school's SEN policy.

Also of relevance to children with SEN are the elements of the 1988 Education Act which enable the delegation of funding from LEAs to schools. Specifically, in those LEAs which delegate SEN funding to schools, this means that resources to meet SEN may be purchased directly by schools, and thus schools are able to make choices over the detailed provision they make and which service they prefer to use.

In short, therefore, there have been clear legislative developments which encourage pupil participation, involving children with SEN in their assessments and plans made for them, and which stress the importance of listening to children's views about their education and schooling.

Recent educational developments

It is probably fair to say that the impact of the Children Act and the Criminal Justice Act have been greater upon those working within social services departments than schools. Within schools, none the less, there exist initiatives to increase children's participation. These include pupil councils, pupil profiling, children's sections of progress reports, or end-of-term/end-of-year reports (in which the child is invited to comment about his or her progress), creative prefect schemes in which the student leadership role is enhanced constructively through training and systematic organizational support, children's views asked about the running of the school, as well as individual child contracts and agreements. Unfortunately, there is relatively little published literature from which it is possible to measure the climate nationally. It is possible to conclude, from visiting a wide range of schools, that although developments are patchy, there is a general trend in the direction of increasing pupil participation, slowly but steadily.

The Code of Practice is likely to have a significant impact on such developments, which will be monitored through school inspections and the working of the new SEN Tribunals.

The history of child participation nationally is possibly typified by three main stages. First, children were to be seen and not heard; they were dealt with as passive objects who should be instructed. This was certainly the view in the last century. The second phase, which is difficult to date, but probably emerged very slowly during the early part of this century, was depicted by the gradually increased involvement of children in everyday life, and at school in active learning and being offered some albeit minimal choices. The third phase (starting at the present time) is characterized by children being given a considerable say in the way things are planned.

It could well be that, at this stage, children are initially given too much voice, and that a correction occurs, to arrive at a balanced approach. For example, this appears to be happening in the area of child abuse. As soon as child testimony began to be taken seriously, there seemed to be a belief by some professionals that all child witnesses should be ascribed greater powers of memory and reliability than adults. This may have led to false accusations of child abuse by adults, and to public interest in the so-called phenomenon of 'false memory syndrome' whereby children report, sometimes following therapy, having been abused many years earlier.

Clifford (1993) queried why the research, which showed very clearly that children were in fact poorer witnesses than adults, should have been ignored. He concluded that the social milieu dictated what knowledge was acceptable.

Most recently, there appears to be a backlash, with teacher unions and some family voluntary groups, television programmes and journalists advocating a more cautious approach. Clearly we need to arrive at a balanced view which gives everybody a fair hearing.

It would appear to us that schools are very broadly a short step into phase three, with some considerable scope for further initiatives. However, there is doubtless wide variation between schools, as there is between families.

It is our view that whilst advocating the rights of the child, and listening very carefully to what children say, we should never forget that they are children, still growing, developing and learning, and that adults, professionals and others have a proper duty of care to act in the best interest of the child, to ensure his or her welfare. Listening sincerely to children is not the same as simply doing what they ask.

Lindsay (1992) helpfully describes three distinctive strands of thinking about children's rights. He explains that, the *protectionist* approach, rooted in the nineteenth century, sees adults as guardians or protectors, and its campaigners worked to remove the worst conditions for children and ensure their proper welfare. The *liberationist* approach stressed the need for children to empower themselves, with proponents of this approach setting up free schools and campaigning for the abolition of age limits, and for children to have the same rights as adults (such as the right to vote, work, to choose where they live, to choose whether or not to attend school, and to have sexual freedoms). Not surprisingly, such an approach has been open to the criticism that it fails to appreciate the special protection children need, and for ignoring the child development evidence. The *pragmatist* approach has attempted a compromise, wishing to provide opportunities for children to express their views and progressively to take on a greater decision-making role, but to do so in the light of their development. The UN Convention, UK legislation and indeed the views of the authors of this chapter would appear to fall within the pragmatist approach.

Recent changes within SEN

As indicated earlier, there have been significant changes in the field of SEN, both in attitude and legislation. Policies of integrating such children in mainstream schools have strengthened and gathered support among many professionals, and parents, and the legislation has reflected this trend.

The 1993 Education Act, which replaces the 1981 Education Act, requires the Secretary of State to publish a Code of Practice for the identification and assessment of SEN, and stresses the importance of pupil involvement throughout the whole assessment process. Sections 2.34 to 2.38 of the Code of Practice (pages 14-15) highlight the importance of involving the child in any assessment and intervention. It states that :

> The effectiveness of any assessment and intervention will be influenced by the involvement and interest of the child and young person concerned. (2.34)

The Code goes on to outline the practical and moral benefits of involving children in their individual educational programmes (IEPs) and decisions about provisions being planned for them. The important moral point is made that children do have a right to be heard. The Code advises schools that they should make

> every effort to identify the ascertainable views and wishes of the child or young person about his or her current and future education

and elaborates this advice, by explaining that:

> Positive pupil involvement is unlikely to happen spontaneously. Careful attention, guidance and encouragement will be required to help pupils respond relevantly and fully. Young people are more likely to respond positively to intervention programmes if they fully understand the rationale for their involvement and if they are given some personal responsibility for their own progress. Schools should, for example, discuss the purpose of a particular assessment arrangement with the child; invite comments from the child; and consider the use of pupil reports and systematic feedback to the child concerned. Many children with SEN have little self-confidence and low self-esteem. Involving children in tracking their own progress within a programme designed to meet their particular learning or behavioural difficulty can contribute to an improved self image and greater self confidence.(2.36)

In addition, under the 1993 Education Act, each school must develop its own SEN policy, and this will clearly need to include procedures in line with the Code, or at least ensure that professionals have due regard to, and do not ignore the Code.

At the time of writing, such legislation is literally within its first few weeks of implementation, but judging by professional interest, research interest and requests for training, it is our view that positive developments likely to increase the active involvement of pupils in assessment, in IEPs and in their schooling generally, are assured.

Increasing pupil self-advocacy and self-advocacy in schools

In this section, following a brief literature review of some relevant action projects and initiatives, we will outline some of the key outcomes from the Waltham Forest Pupil Involvement Project in which the first author, together with colleagues, has been developing tools and techniques to increase the active involvement of pupils in their education and school life. A major outcome has been the publication of a Student Report for children with SEN. Some other work to prepare children for more active participation in decision making, using an example from the courts, namely the Child Witness Pack will also be reviewed. Our primary focus in this section, is upon projects which encourage children to speak up for themselves, or pupil self-advocacy.

There is relatively limited evidence of research into pupil involvement or pupil self-advocacy in education in the UK. The few studies which have been carried out, albeit with small samples, or those which suggest ideas for the future, are nevertheless of interest in setting the scene.

Armstrong et al. (1993) examined the role of children in assessments and found that children's contributions were often minimal. These workers felt that this was due to a combination of clinical difficulties in ascertaining pupil's views and constraints in the ways professionals conceptualized children's needs. They also felt that children's beliefs about the assessment process and the professionals involved had a significant impact upon their responses.

Their study was based upon the experience of 29 children aged 5 to 16 being formally assessed and a further 18 children in an off-site unit for behavioural difficulties. Some children reported feeling anxious about the assessment, they were often unaware of the decision-making process, unclear about the roles of different professionals, and unsure about the outcome. Considerable misinterpretations were evident, with some children not feeling able to express their views during interviews.

Paul Cooper (1993) studied the views of pupils in two residential special schools, finding that they most valued the respite, relationships and opportunities provided in their school. He points out the difficulties in ascertaining pupil's views, and some possible factors influencing their answers, such as the pupil's perceptions of the interviewer, the purpose of the discussion and the future audience.

Cooper makes some practical suggestions for interviewers. He argues that, in order to obtain honest responses, they should make explicit the purpose of the meeting, ensure confidentiality, be non-judgmental, accepting and show positive regard for the pupil, exploring openly any reservations the child might have about the process. The meeting itself, he says, should be private, uninterrupted, and conducted in a style which involves open-ended questions, an agenda which is shaped by the concerns of the child, uses pupil vocabulary, and should be voluntary. The interviewer should communicate interest, empathy, positive regard, patience and move at an appropriate pace, ending with warmth and appreciation.

From another stance, some workers have attempted to advocate pupils' views through advocacy and self-advocacy services. Dalrymple (1993), the director of Advice, Advocacy and Self-advocacy and Representation Services for Children, gives an account of the operation which was launched in 1992. She explains that some 200 requests for assistance from children were received during the past year, mainly from children in residential care. This service provides professional independent advocates, and telephone advocacy and self-advocacy. It is based in Manchester and has a freephone number (0800 616101). From the cases described it is clear that many children had derived considerable benefit from the service. Dalrymple views the most important components of the service as it being independent, young person focused, unconstrained by divided loyalties and capable of assuring confidentiality to children.

In a similar vein, Cathy Cooper (1992) has pioneered a self-advocacy group called People First for people with learning difficulties, to take control of their lives. Most members are adults but there are plans to involve younger people, starting with a new project for 16 to 25 year olds. This organization has also campaigned to change the image of disability, and promotes advocacy and self-advocacy, encouraging people to present their own views directly.

Arguing that standard complaints procedures rarely work, the Local Authority in Leicester has appointed a Children's Rights Officer. In an interview with Bartlett (1989), Mike Lindsay, the Officer concerned, outlined his role as the first such Officer. It appears that the publicity and approach had led to the success of the scheme in assisting more children who would otherwise not have come forward for help. Nevertheless, Lindsay depicts the inevitable resistance to such posts, which some see as a threat to their professional integrity. Since 1989, more Children's Rights Officers have been appointed, and there are an estimated 10 in the country (Murray, 1993), plus what appears to be a developing professional group, with its own association and distinct training needs.

Such developments have arisen within social services rather than education departments and appear to have been targeted toward children in care. Do we need similar schemes targeting school pupils? Clearly, who will use such a service will very much depend upon how it is publicised, marketed and presented.

The Waltham Forest Pupil Involvement Project

During the past 10 to 12 years, the first author, together with colleagues within the Waltham Forest Educational Psychology Service a series of trainee educational psychologists and teachers, and education department officers have carried out a number of different projects and action research initiatives in order to explore practical ways of increasing the active involvement of children in their education.

Such projects have led to the publication of a Child Report (Gersch and Cutting, 1985) for children in a Social Services Residential Assessment Centre, who were being assessed by the social services so that future residential and educational plans could be made for them. A Student Report (Gersch et al., 1993; Gersch and Holgate, 1994), is completed by children with SEN outlining the child's perspective, and a Pupil Self Rating Scale (Gersch, 1990) is provided for use in the classroom. Children are invited to judge their own work effort and achievements.

A Secondary School Systems Project (Gersch and Noble, 1991) aimed to change a secondary school system and had, at its heart, pupils included in the working parties and central to the decision-making machinery. This project was set up to examine the causes of truancy in the school, and invited students to give their perspectives on the problem and ideas about solutions. Many practical proposals followed, including the setting up of a Pupil Council, a student newsletter and suggestions for extra-curricular activities. The main point, however, was that pupils were involved in changing the school system. A subsequent evaluation indicated that, apart from some positive practical outcomes, the headteacher felt that communication within the whole school seemed to have improved as had relationships between staff and pupils.

Research into pupils' views of their headteachers and school leadership also revealed interesting data about what children wanted from their headteachers (Gersch, 1992). They clearly wanted someone to turn to in difficulty, someone who could adjudicate fairly, and someone who knew them well.

At Borough Council level, a decision was made, following wide consultation locally, to highlight the importance of pupil involvement and listening to children's views, as a core principle in the Borough's policy on SEN.

Other reports and pupil booklets which have been used include a Student Report for children being assessed under the 1981 Education Act, at the 13+ reassessment stage (Gersch, 1987), and a booklet for the use of excluded pupils (Gersch and Nolan, 1994; Nolan and Sigston, 1993). Details of these initiatives are described in Gersch (1987;1990; 1992), Gersch, et al., (op. cit.), Gersch and Nolan(op. cit.).

Perhaps the key point to make is that although the techniques which were developed are useful in their own right, they are simply vehicles and tools for children to use. The aim has always been to empower children and magnify their voices, or create opportunities for staff to listen. Many of the Child Reports and Student Reports have been changed and amended over time, in the light of evaluations (with staff and, of course, children) and no booklet or device is regarded as other than a temporary technique which should be varied flexibly to enable the individual child to respond readily and comfortably.

During the first project, (Gersch and Cutting, 1985) it was found necessary to provide clear instructions for adult helpers, some of whom were treating the completion of the form as a formal test and, for example, when reading out the questions to children unable to read, felt restricted to the actual wording. Our subsequent instructions for adult helpers remind them that the aim is to obtain as true a picture of the young person's views as possible, and to encourage free expression, by explaining any unfamiliar words and remaining impartial, taking care to avoid implanting their own (adult) views. Of course, many children will be able to complete the form without external help.

Although some teachers have argued that having a separate report completed by the child may not be necessary, our experience has shown that a written record adds weight to the pupil's view, it ensures greater focus and discussion than might otherwise take place, and children themselves both value and enjoy the opportunity, most often stating helpful and sensible things. One young person, aged 14, told us several years ago that this was the first time anyone had asked him to comment upon his school plans and lessons.

The latest Student Report is an attractive booklet for children to complete. There are seven main sections:

School
Special needs
Friends
Out of school
Feelings
The future
Anything else to add.

Children are invited to write down what they like and dislike in each area, what help they feel they need and what plans they would like to make. In the light of experience we have changed the wording, presentation and format. Overall, children say that they enjoy completing the form, they find it helpful and they tend to write down interesting things, in a very clear way, which professionals have found very useful in decision making. The projects described fall into three main categories:

a) the development of child or student reports or booklets
b) action research into what children think about their schools and wish to change, and
c) initiatives to include children in the decision making within their class (in respect of their own learning) or whole school.

Overall, each project has gone through several phases, as follows:

1.   Convincing the adults of the benefits
2   Initiating the new vehicle, device or procedure

3.   Developing the device with colleagues
4.   Piloting the device with children
5.   Evaluating the processes or techniques
6.   Changing the device or procedure in the light of
          experience.

All of our experience points to real benefits in involving pupils in their assessments and schooling, and typically for the principle to be adopted again in future work being undertaken by the school and teachers. What is also interesting to note is that such pupil involvement initiatives have taken place at several levels:

The Council Level
The whole school level
The classroom level
The individual child level

Although our student reports have been published and are available to colleagues, and indeed have been used nationally (Gersch and Holgate, 1994) as has the booklet for excluded pupils (Nolan and Sigston, 1993), professionals may need to develop and adapt their own materials in the light of local circumstances and contexts.

The NSPCC Child Witness Pack

A somewhat different approach to increasing the involvement of children is through using educative and preparatory material to ensure that when children's views are invited they can respond effectively. Although this example relates to preparing children for court appearances, no doubt teachers could have a key role in undertaking some of the preparatory work, together with other professionals.

There is evidence that children are being asked to attend court more frequently than in the past, due to changes in legal procedures and the wish to include the views of children in both criminal and civil cases. Consequently, the NSPCC in conjunction with the Home Office, the Lord Chancellor's department, the Crown Prosecution Service, the Department of Health, Childline, the Children's Society, the Children's Legal centre, and the National Children's Bureau have produced an excellent pack of materials, based on research and examples of good practice, called The Child Witness Pack (Plotnikoff, 1993).

There are materials which can be used for child witnesses aged 5 to 9, others for those aged 10 to 15 and information for parents and carers. The material is colourful, accessible for children and doubtless helps them prepare for the daunting experience. The aim of the pack is to help reduce the stress of courtroom attendance, as well as to safeguard the welfare of children throughout the case. It provides children with practical support, so that they will feel more confident and equipped to appear in court.

The pack can be used by teachers and other professionals to prepare children for court, through the pictures and topics included for discussion, quizzes and games. This has been utilised in a secondary school by Ruth Lockhart and comments about the pack sought from children, teachers and educational psychologists (Gersch *et al.*, in preparation).

Perhaps the important point to make is that when one is considering ways of increasing the active involvement of children in any institution, procedure or operation, thought needs to be given to *preparing* the child. Recently, there was a press report of a barrister working with a child with Lego to demonstrate the layout of the courtroom and what happens, an idea which has much to commend it.

None of us can contribute properly unless we have enough knowledge of the situation and indeed sufficient confidence to wish to contribute. The parallel is probably adult attendance at case conferences; if parents for example feel unfamiliar with the rules and conventions of the process and aims of a meeting, and thus experience anxiety, their ability to contribute effectively may be diminished. Children may similarly need to receive preparation to participate effectively.

The role of allied professionals in respect of child advocacy and self-advocacy in SEN

Under the 1993 Education Act, LEAs are obliged to collect written Advice from a number of different professionals in order to carry out a statutory assessment for those children who appear to have significant SEN, which cannot ordinarily be met within the available resources of the school.

Typically, LEAs employ an officer or head of special needs section who will be responsible for contacting every professional who is involved with the child, to request this written Advice. Usually, such Advices are submitted to an LEA SEN Panel which is charged with making a decision about whether or not to produce a Statement and if so, to draft its content.

In this section we will report the findings of a recent survey, carried out by the second author, of the attitudes and practices of a small sample of these professionals. In order to ascertain current practice of professionals working with children with SEN, a questionnaire and interviews were used, in September 1994. The sample, although small, covered the range of professionals who might be asked to submit Advice to the LEA for a statutory assessment and allowed the authors to gain a general flavour of the current perspectives of these professions with regard to involving children in their assessments, actively seeking their views on child advocacy and self-advocacy.

The questionnaire and interview covered four areas. The first section focused on the professional's personal views and concerns about seeking the views of children. The second dealt with specific methods or techniques to draw out children's views. Section three looked at attitudes and developments within the profession as a whole and section four invited respondents to add any other comments or suggestions that they felt relevant. The professionals interviewed included an educational psychologist, specialist teacher, physiotherapist, consultant community paediatrician, education social worker, speech therapist, child psychiatrist and social worker. One professional from each discipline was selected on the basis of their knowledge, experience and ability to comment upon overall developments and practice within their particular field.

The Educational Psychologist

The educational psychologist (EP) had a specific allocation of schools within an LEA and described her role as one of giving professional advice to teachers, parents and the LEA about children with SEN. She felt that EPs were often seen by children as 'sympathetic and impartial outsiders' and as such were well placed to listen to the concerns and ideas of children, which she considered was vital.

The psychologist always made sure that children were completely clear and indeed happy about her meeting with them and encouraged children to ask questions freely throughout the session. She specifically asked children about their concerns and also why they thought others were worried about them and indeed included their views in her written Advice.

In terms of feeding back findings and recommendations, the EP did this directly with the child and used this session as an opportunity to emphasise positive aspects and abilities of the child, whilst including areas where help was needed. She stated that her aim was to leave the child with higher self-esteem than before. Although parents were not present during her sessions with the child, with the exception of pre-school children, the psychologist always sought parental permission. In the event of a difference of opinion between child and parent, the psychologist saw her role as one of mediator, trying to ensure that each heard the other's point of view. It was interesting to note on the topic of a child's involvement in their annual review, that the psychologist felt that many children found these meetings too intimidating and felt more comfortable expressing their views outside the meeting to a trusted teacher or classroom assistant.

When asked about the views of the profession as a whole in terms of child involvement, the psychologist felt that EPs always focused on the child; respecting and listening to children was a solid thread which ran throughout the profession and indeed was a feature in their training. Interestingly, she felt that although the Children Act had very little impact on work in her profession, the 1993 Education Act and Code of Practice would encourage a clearer and earlier identification of children with SEN and that specific and formal recording at the school-based stages of assessment would need to reflect the child's views.

When asked about changes needed within the profession, the psychologist felt that it would be helpful if it were a statutory requirement for EPs to spend more time with children. Severe constraints on time currently left little opportunity for psychologists to build a trusting relationship with the child. Overall, she felt that she did act as an advocate for the child but would welcome a system whereby the child was allocated a specific advocate, similar to a guardian *ad litem*.

The Specialist Teacher

The next person interviewed was a specialist teacher who worked for the Support for Learning Service in an LEA. Her responsibilities included a caseload of children in mainstream schools whom she taught on a sessional basis, and in addition, as a team leader, she also trained special classroom assistants. She saw her role as being completely child-centred and therefore felt that listening to children was of key importance. The teacher felt that a solution-focused approach to teaching was most helpful, particularly for children with SEN. This approach offered opportunities for children to be directly involved in their individual learning programmes, for example by setting work targets and logging their own progress.

This respondent always explained her role to the child and specifically recorded both the child's and parents' views, particularly in her initial assessment report. When discussing a possible difference of opinion between the child and parent, it was felt that sometimes parents of children with SEN could be negative, dismissive and underestimate their child's achievements. She believed that she had an important part to play by showing parents concrete evidence of the child's good work and maybe explaining that even very small achievements should be valued. This is clearly an advocacy role.

In terms of attitudes within the profession as a whole, the teacher felt that, sadly, there was a long way to go. She indicated that some teachers paid lip-service to the idea of children's involvement. Some didn't think it appropriate and others were actually disturbed about the notion of seeking children's views. She thought that children's involvement in their education should be structured and formalised so that it became good working practice for all teachers. This would hopefully close the gap between 'the dream and reality' that she feels exists in the profession.

On the question of changes following the Children Act, the teacher felt, as did the educational psychologist, that this Act had little impact on schools. Of interest, however, was her view that this may have been due to timing. During the period of 1989 - 1991 there had been many new initiatives and changes in schools and many teachers felt overwhelmed by them.

In terms of whether she could act as an advocate for children, the teacher had mixed feelings. On the one hand it was true to say that SEN teachers seem to take a lead in fighting for children whom the system may have failed. Alternatively, there is a view that because new initiatives in schools have veered towards systems work and whole-school approaches, it is quite possible for an individual child's voice to go unheard in the school environment.

The Physiotherapist

The physiotherapist interviewed was responsible for the assessment and treatment of children in a variety of settings which included a school for severe learning difficulties, a Child Development Unit and mainstream schools.

When interviewing the physiotherapist it became clear that this profession lagged behind the education sector in terms of seeking the child's view. Although the physiotherapist agreed with the principle of involving children in their assessments and treatment, in reality there were many limitations on this. Many of the children seen by her had severe learning difficulties and she felt that they were unable to express a view. In addition, children with such severe difficulties were often unaware of their disability. A further limitation is that in the medical field it is sometimes necessary for children to receive treatment that may be unpleasant and which they may resist. In those cases, seeking the child's views would not be seen as appropriate. However, the physiotherapist always took great care to talk things through with children, explain why certain treatments had to be carried out and try to plan goals together; naturally, this depended on the child's level of comprehension.

Although there were not clear guidelines for the profession, the physiotherapist felt that within medicine as a whole there was definitely a move towards more democratic treatment of patients which in time would include children. She did not feel that she acted as an advocate for children but did add that on occasion she had represented their views and concerns in discussion with their parents.

The Community Paediatrician

The consultant community paediatrician described her responsibilities as including pre-school child health surveillance, school health service, medical advice for fostering and adoption and advice to the LEA about children with SEN.

Although this doctor felt that it was important to listen to children's views, she felt that it was also important to let them know that she wouldn't always be able to do what they wanted. She also felt strongly that young children up to the age of 12 or 13 did not have the benefit of experience or knowledge to appreciate or have influence over what must happen to them. Because of her feelings about this, when meeting with families, all her comments were directed to the parents who had to be present at the examination. In her practice, the paediatrician used the 'Gillick competency' guidelines which meant that she would only deal directly with young people when they had reached teenage years.

On the subject of change following the Children Act, as with other respondents, the doctor felt it had limited impact on the medical profession. However, she felt that changes were necessary to alter the 'mind-set' of doctors who were not always very good at communicating at all, let alone with children. She thought that medical students should be trained to talk and listen to children.

In terms of her adopting an advocacy role, the paediatrician felt that she often acted as advocate for the family as a whole, rather than for an individual child, for example to plead their case to the Housing Department to help secure better accommodation.

The Education Social Worker

The education social worker (ESW) described himself as being responsible for maintaining an acceptable level of attendance in his allocated mainstream schools and for supporting the placements in a special school for children with emotional and behavioural difficulties (EBD).

He was very enthusiastic about hearing children's views and in fact saw this as being one of his key roles. He felt that all children had an acute sense of wanting to be heard and to be treated fairly. However, it was not always easy to extract children's views and this needed to be done skilfully and sensitively. In his practice he always sought to talk to a child in the place where she or he felt most comfortable and he aimed to establish a relaxed trusting relationship. He made a point of asking the child their views at several points during the interview, to establish that the child was important and paramount in the whole process.

As far as the profession as a whole was concerned, it was clear from his responses that ascertaining the views of the child are entrenched in ESW practice. In addition, the legislation that he worked under, for example the Children Act and the 1993 Education Act emphasised the importance of listening to the child.

Indeed, an Education Supervision Order necessitates that evidence is shown to indicate that both the child's and the parents' views have been sought.

In terms of future changes, the ESW thought that his fellow professionals were well placed to act as advocates for the child and to have a fundamental role in ascertaining their views.

The Speech Therapist

The speech therapist felt that it was important to listen to children in order to gain their interest and cooperation Her particular responsibility included a general caseload of children under five and therefore the ability of children to comprehend was felt to be the greatest limitation for seeking their views. However, the speech therapist used the technique of gauging the child's wishes from his or her behaviour when they were unable to express themselves verbally.

Another technique used widely in the profession was that of open-ended questions which encouraged a shy or reluctant child to express themselves and to respond with more than 'yes' or 'no'. This has been very successful and is thought to be a less threatening mode of communicating to children than direct questions.

On the question of explaining her role and the purpose of the assessment to the child, the speech therapist used her judgement with each child. She felt that very often the child was unaware of a problem and in such cases her examination was often done by clinical observation alone.

Within the profession as a whole, the speech therapist felt that there was a great emphasis on looking at the child holistically and therefore their views were fundamental. The Children Act had made no apparent difference to her working practice but she was aware that her managers in the Speech Therapy Service were looking at their policies in the light of the 1993 Education Act and Code of Practice.

The speech therapist had an interesting perspective on the question of being an advocate for the child. She felt very strongly that speech therapists were in an unusual position of being able to link medical, educational and psychological aspects of the child. She felt that everything about a child is reflected through their speech and therefore the speech therapist has a unique role to 'pull things together' for the parents and child.

The Child Psychiatrist

The psychiatrist was a consultant in adolescent and child psychiatry and had been in practice for 20 years. Her responsibilities included the treatment of children and families who presented with a range of difficulties which caused concern, and supervision and training of colleagues in the Child Mental Health Team.

The psychiatrist felt that although she listened carefully to children, it was important for them to know that she would not just 'do what they wanted'. She added that sometimes children expressed views which may not be in their best interests and that it was her task to judge what was in the child's best interests whilst taking their wishes into account.

Although the psychiatrist felt that her focus was on the child, she usually discussed her findings and treatment plan with the family as a whole. Whilst she was aware of the Children Act and 1993 Education Act and Code of Practice the psychiatrist felt that neither had an impact on her professional practice.

In terms of acting as an advocate for the child, the psychiatrist did feel well placed to express the child's views, but more often acted on behalf of the family as a whole.

The Social Worker

The social worker interviewed worked as part of a Child and Family Area Team and dealt with child protection, children who were 'looked after' by the local authority and children in need. She felt it was vital to listen to the views of children, but as part of an overall framework which took additional information and the views of others into account. However, she expressed some very strong concerns about striking the right balance between seeking a child's view and giving the impression to the child that she or he was responsible for making all the decisions. She cited a worrying example of a very disturbed 9 year old boy who was dragged off the roof of a building to attend his case conference and present his views. The social worker felt very strongly that this was totally inappropriate and moreover constituted an emotional abuse of the child.

When asked specifically about inviting a child to express a view as part of their assessment, the social worker felt that she would if she were sure that the child had all the information and was aware of the possible options before coming to a view.

On the question of dealing with a possible difference between the parent and child, the social worker felt that her response would depend very much on her professional view and why she thought that they were taking a particular stance. Very often, she would try to obtain parental support in order to present a united front to the child. At other times, it was necessary to try to make variations to plans and accommodations so that compromises could be agreed. Overall, however, she felt that when either party was faced with concrete evidence, agreement could usually be reached.

In terms of the profession as a whole, the social worker felt that attitudes about taking children seriously were 'patchy'. She was aware that some social workers could take a rather rigid and inflexible line. However, since the Children Act, social workers were obliged to ascertain the views of children and this was general practice.

It was felt that the Cleveland Report had the greatest impact on the profession as a whole. All social workers are now aware that cases can be brought to court by children themselves who are able to consult solicitors in their own right. Social workers are aware that all court reports must have a record of the views of the child and they are mindful of this when writing up their report in case it eventually comes before the court.

In terms of changes required in the profession, the social worker felt that more training was needed on communicating with children, especially those with special needs. She reiterated her point about the great skill and sensitivity needed when ascertaining the views of the child so as not to make them feel totally responsible for decisions made.

On the question of acting as an advocate for the child, she felt that the best and most appropriate advocate was the parent but that she would take on that role wholeheartedly when she felt that 'no one else was looking out for the child.'

Summary

Whilst the sample was small, the impression gained was that the views and ideas expressed were likely to be representative of the professions concerned and to have wider generalisability. The main findings were as follows:

a) Overall, the professionals felt that the child's view was important and should be sought where possible.

b) Differences existed between professional groups, with a tendency from those with a social work or educational background, rather than those with a medical background, to place greater emphasis on involving the child. Medical specialists tended to give greater weight to the family view, the needs (rather than preferences) of children, and to feel that children younger than about 12 years usually lacked sufficient maturity to understand the consequences of decisions.

c) Important points were made about the gap between the ideal and reality, in that professionals might wish to involve children actively, in theory, and indeed believe that they do so, whilst in reality children might not feel actively engaged. The study by Armstrong *et al.* (1993) indicated that there were misunderstandings between how children perceived their interviews with EPs, for example, and how the latter construed situations.

d) The point was also made by the social worker that one had to be careful in striking a balance between listening to children, and placing them in an invidious and unrealistic position of feeling over-burdened with decision-making responsibilities. It was argued that the child's views should be considered as part of an overall framework which included the views of others, such as parents and teachers.

e) Most professionals felt that they could advocate the child's views, although there were differences between professional groups, and there were limits to how far they could act independently.

This last finding will be discussed in more detail in the next section, when we explore some professional dilemmas and constraints to advocacy and self-advocacy.

Some professional dilemmas and constraints to advocacy and self-advocacy

There are serious constraints and problems in professionals taking on an advocacy and self-advocacy role. These might be considered under five headings, although they are certainly not intended to be exhaustive.

a) Employment conditions

Most professionals are employed or paid by someone to undertake their professional service; this may be the Education Department, the Health Authority, an NHS Trust, or even the family itself, on a private basis. Professionals may find themselves under pressure from their employer to make what are regarded as realistic or economic recommendations, rather than cause embarrassment.

Conflicts can arise between the interests, say, of the family, the child and the professional. It would be a pretence to maintain that conflicts of interest could not occur. Perhaps, just as insurance agents now have to state the source of any commission, professionals will at some time in the future be duty-bound to explain their employment status and the limits to which they might act as a child or family advocate.

b) Freedom of expression

In similar vein, professionals might be restricted in the lengths to which they are able to go to support a child's view or preferences. Would they feel able to join a child in litigation against their employer for example? Would they be accused of using 'insider information' if they countered the view of their employer? Would they ever be trusted again if they did so? Would they be regarded as ' trouble'? These are hard questions which professionals might face. They also might depend upon the real attitudes of the employer and their commitment to professional liberty.

The question which would face a professional advocating the views of the child, is rarely *are* you able to do this, but rather, *to what degree* are you able to advocate the view, and *at what point* do you withdraw? And of course, at what point do you place your future employment or relationships in jeopardy?

Ethically, every professional will need to act in accordance with certain standards, in the interests of the child, but the real dilemmas occur at the borderline and in the hazy area. There is often a tension between purist and pragmatic decision making, since we all live in the real world in which compromises have to be made.

c) Negative attitudes of others

Professionals advocating for children will undoubtedly face the challenge of other adults who question the validity of taking children's views seriously, arguing that adults know best, and children lack the necessary ability, experience, maturity or knowledge.

We would argue that even very young children can often surprise us in their perceptiveness and insights, and children and young people with the most severe learning problems are able to express preferences. Indeed, the challenge is to provide the right conditions and ethos to tap these views, the onus being on adults to provide a climate of trust, confidence, openness and understanding so that children do express themselves freely. This is no easy task, and there is much to be learnt from our counselling colleagues about how to listen in a non-judgmental way.

However, it may not be unhelpful for professionals acting as child advocates to expect to be seen by colleagues, at times, as adopting a naive and unrealistic position, and to be ready with some counter arguments!

d) Parent-child conflicts

Issues can arise where there appear to be conflicts of views between children and their parents, particularly with adolescents. Compromises might be pursued successfully, but if this is not possible, one could argue that each professional will need to arrive at their own judgement about what is in the child's best interest.

e) Ascertaining the child's view

This probably is the most difficult part of the exercise. The components of effective listening appear to be time, space, empathy, openness, trust, warmth, with professionals offering a non-judgmental approach and communicating that it is safe to express views freely. One only needs to think of the people who oneself searches out to talk over problems with, and indeed those whom one wishes to avoid, to identify the qualities required of 'good listeners'.

It is also important to stress that children's views will change, develop and be refined in the light of discussion, exploration, new data and perhaps experiences. We should therefore be encouraging children to try new things, visit and see things for themselves, *before* making up their mind. We all perhaps need to accept that it is alright to change our minds, in the light of such developments - a view that is sometimes perceived as a weakness rather than a strength.

Whilst we are sure there are other obstacles to advocacy and self-advocacy that professionals might face, we do feel that forewarned is forearmed. Further, we would argue that the best advocate is ultimately the child, and thus professionals might be serving the child's cause better through empowering the child to respond in his or her own words, and working to open up channels of such communication, rather than aiming always to speak for the child.

Conclusions

Whilst much is happening in the area of pupil advocacy and self-advocacy, and it seems as though we are now poised for a spurt in school-based and educational initiatives, there are real professional constraints which need be faced honestly and openly.

We have reviewed a number of techniques, reports and projects aimed at increasing the active participation of children in assessment and their school life generally, but the point must be stressed that attitudes and ethos are more important than techniques. Further, listening properly to children requires qualities, arrangements, skills and attitudes which must be in place, if any technique is to be effective and valid.

We have also argued that we should be working towards encouraging child self-advocacy, providing tools, communication channels, power and training to children. This would enable them to express their own views assertively, clearly and sensitively, and gain skills during their school careers which will be of value to them for the rest of their lives.

Acknowledgements

We are grateful to all the staff, children and trainee EPs who have taken part in the projects described above, and to the LEA officers and other professionals for their assistance. We are particularly indebted to Carmel Littleton, Sarah Gale, Jacqui Tasker, David Hough, Ruth Caudwell, Anne Marie Desiree, Aparna Bhonsle and Celia Parker for their contributions.

However, the views expressed in this chapter remain those of the authors' alone and do not necessarily represent those of the authority, schools or services in which the work took place, or where they are currently employed.

SECTION THREE:

PROFESSIONAL DEVELOPMENT FOR ADVOCACY AND SELF-ADVOCACY

The professional development of those who work with children who have special needs should provide a supportive framework within which teachers can explore their individual and collective feelings concerning pupil empowerment. Understanding the implications of listening to children enables practical actions to be justified.

This final section traces some potential themes for in-service training. In doing so it outlines a number of principles for promoting pupil-empowerment which, without question, should form an integral part of the professional development portfolio of all teachers.

Chapter 3.1

DEVELOPING AN INDIVIDUAL APPROACH

Of all human professions, teaching has perhaps been most open to the vagaries of public and political opinion. We have all been children, so it is little wonder that everyone feels entitled to offer an opinion about the way in which those who teach children should behave (Barton, 1991). Being a parent reinforces this interest. Formal education is, moreover, a fundamental aspect of cultural transmission, and in consequence it has been customary for governments in England to take an active interest in the way in which student-teachers are trained - certainly more so than other professions, such as lawyers, doctors or dentists. This involvement is maintained throughout the professional lives of teachers, notably by the controls exercised by government on the opportunities for, and the content of, in-service training (INSET).

It is hardly surprising, therefore, that the teaching profession has developed a high degree of self-scrutiny, cynicism or even resistance towards intervention in its training practices. It often seems as though the profession can do little that is right: if GCSE results are too good then educational standards must be falling; if children are eating too many sweets teachers are held responsible for not providing adequate coverage of health education within the pastoral curriculum; and if standards of literacy are reported to be in decline teachers are simply not doing their job. The frequent sensationalist coverage in the media of the alleged professional incompetence of some teachers is now commonplace. The picture generated, therefore, is one of an embattled profession inclined to retreat behind procedural barriers which inhibit the development of advocacy and self-advocacy opportunities.

Recent years have witnessed an unparalleled change in teachers' professional lives, encompassing 'reforms' in curriculum practice and initial teacher education (which has been reformulated as 'training'). Concerns over job security, re-orientation and extension of working practices and changes in inspection have not eased the sense of job-frustration felt by many (Barton, 1991). Additionally, the demands made on classroom teachers to conform to the ideological requirements inherent in these changes are substantial. One example of this has been the pressure exerted on the profession by central government to accept a rigid assessment regime for the National Curriculum. Another is the move towards a return of streaming, which has been seen as a way of ensuring good academic performance. Both are ultimately counter-productive to the development of advocacy and self-advocacy.

Amidst these concerns, teachers have to meet the routine demands of their occupation. Frequently they have to work in less than perfect conditions, sometimes with difficult children and with inadequate resources. Since 1988 teachers have also had to adapt to the chameleon that is the National Curriculum, attempting to make sense of Tuesday's amendment to KS 2 English in readiness for its implementation the following Wednesday. Official impetus in INSET has been substantially directed towards the structural aspects of recent educational changes. Thus increasing emphasis has been placed upon matters relating to curriculum content, assessment procedures, 'control' of behaviour and aspects of school governance, to the exclusion of the more process-orientated focus of the profession. Peter (1991), for example, suggested that

> in-service training in the National Curriculum should remain a high priority. Subject content, task differentiation, classroom organisation and management are particularly important (p. 162).

Would it be disingenuous to note that pupil-participation is studiously avoided? Thomas (1993), in summarising this way of thinking 'professionally', states that

> The 'value for money concept' in in-service training could mean an increasing emphasis upon skills-related training with easily measurable outcomes with little room for courses of a more flexible character. (p.117).

Significantly, too, there have been fundamental changes in the way in which INSET in SEN has been approached in the 1990s. The SEN coordinator and individual subject teachers, having been allocated specific responsibilities for SEN, have had to come to terms with the increasingly procedural nature of their work. Considerable focus has been placed upon subject-knowledge and its assessment following the Education Reform Act. Training days in school have frequently concentrated on information about these aspects of the National Curriculum. Little room appears to have been made for the development of more-cooperative approaches in classrooms, probably because they do not give an immediate pay-off. School-based INSET concerned with managing problem behaviour also adopts a largely instrumental, controlling approach. Again this has been the result of the pressure placed upon schools to be seen as orderly places, where discipline is strong and where children who have emotional and behavioural difficulties are 'managed' by a well-defined system of external controls.

It is also the case that, as financial constraints on funding INSET have become more apparent, there has been a reduction in the opportunities for teachers from a range of different schools and LEAs to engage in joint INSET. 'Special Needs in Ordinary Schools' (SENIOS) courses, followed on a day-release basis by teachers from a wide variety of backgrounds and working contexts, have all but disappeared from the INSET landscape. As a result we are left with an impoverished provision, in which 'Recent reports have drawn attention to the danger of re-cycled bad practice' (Thomas, 1993).

In the face of official and societal demands for 'effective' schools, professional development in SEN has failed to encourage child-focussed approaches which allow for greater pupil participation. This is particularly the case where INSET for SEN coordinators is concerned. This group has assumed widespread organisational responsibilities following the publication of the Code of Practice (DfE, 1994a). The Code offers a utilitarian view of the SEN coordinator's job, and deals mainly with the organisation and procedures connected with identification and assessment. The opportunities to generate points for empowerment within the curriculum and the wider social life of the classroom may, therefore, be overshadowed by other demands, an issue emphasised by Gains (1994).

A similar change can be detected in the content of many award-bearing INSET courses provided by universities and colleges. Just as the financing of schools is now prescribed by pupil numbers, institutions involved in the delivery of diploma and masters courses have to recruit and keep students in order to survive. Student evaluation, on the completion of courses, indicates a wish for information-giving rather than a critical reflective analysis - a 'tips for teachers' approach. In order to maintain student numbers institutions are left with little alternative but to adopt a utilitarian stance: education becomes training, in much the same way as initial teacher training (ITT) is the market-led derivitive of initial teacher education (ITE).

Many of the preceding observations apply across most aspects of education. What marks a point of departure from general educational provision, however, is the relative decline in resources available for INSET in SEN. Prior to 1988 the last major piece of SEN education, the 1981 Act, was accompanied by significant support for INSET through LEA funding. It was far easier to obtain release from teaching to attend courses and the necessary funds were available to pay for attendance on both long and short courses. There was a commensurate freedom for teachers to attend INSET sessions on matters less directly relevant to government policy.

The position in the 1990s is more depressing. Opportunities for INSET in SEN have rapidly contracted, partly on account of the demise of the influential LEA-led provision. Current opportunities for INSET frequently exist as responses to policy initiatives from central government. Moreover, it is now common for teachers to fund their own attendance on SEN courses. Teachers involved in SEN (not only coordinators) have had to respond to wholesale changes in the way in which their specialism has been conceptualised and delivered. Many teachers have felt that the only courses worth attending are those which provide them with the means necessary to implement the statutory changes demanded of them. In addition, teachers understandably wish to expand those skills which will be the focus of subsequent OFSTED scrutiny. The current Inspection Manual (OFSTED, 1993b) gives only fleeting acknowledgement of the need to incorporate the views of children who have SEN (DfE, 1993). INSET in SEN, in other words, has become an activity in which it is pragmatic for teachers to participate as opposed to obtaining intrinsic benefit from so doing.

Of course, this picture is overstated, and arguably leans heavily upon the negative aspects of recent developments. But what it does illustrate is the shifting ground that the profession as a whole has occupied over the last few years and which is crystallised in the dilemmas surrounding INSET in SEN. These, when taken with the traditional left-of-centre stance of the profession, may arguably make an imperfect basis for developing an individual approach to empowering children. As has been noted at various points in this volume, giving children opportunities to state opinions is a risk-taking activity, in which there is much potential for misunderstanding. Teachers who may themselves feel under threat, for any of the reasons outlined above, may be ill-prepared or unwilling to promote advocacy and self-advocacy. The present chapter considers some of the dilemmas of INSET in SEN and suggests an agenda by which teachers can develop a personal approach to advocacy in a number of interdependent areas. Each will have significant importance for the growth of opportunities for SEN pupils to participate in their own learning.

If we accept the view offered by Weber (1982) that 'the teacher is the key', a premium must be placed on ensuring that individual classroom teachers are equipped to promote advocacy and self-advocacy. We have suggested that this has been made more difficult because of the occupational stress faced by many teachers. Nevertheless, two overlapping areas of INSET can be noted: firstly, consideration of the so-called hidden curriculum of relationships and daily interactions between teacher and pupils in the classroom as a focus for the teacher's self-examination of his or her own set of belief-systems; secondly, the way in which individual teachers interpret and teach the formal, prescribed curriculum.

Advocacy, self-advocacy and the individual teacher

A starting point for the development of an 'empowered classroom' is that teachers themselves should feel confident, by virtue of their own critical reflection, that they have uncovered the limitations of traditional educational thinking. This is based on control, competition and dogma. To begin this process it is important that teachers have an understanding of 'self'. This includes a reflective understanding of the importance of the way in which they transmit messages to the whole class on an informal basis. In other words, a starting point is the creation of an appropriate classroom 'climate' which fosters a feeling of confidence and well-being, so that children can play some part in controlling their own learning.

This may not be easy to achieve in the prevailing climate of instrumentally-governed INSET in SEN. Adopting a cooperative approach to teaching and learning helps to make classrooms into purposeful centres of learning for *all* children. The professional development portfolio of teachers therefore must include an opportunity to examine their practice and to relate it to the experience of children who have SEN. A reflective, questioning stance to their role in the classroom can help to facilitate this. Senior management teams, for their part, must accept that time needs to be allocated, within the hourage set aside for professional development, for this kind of critical reflection supported by other teachers. Activities which allow classroom teachers to explore their professional responses to the rights of children could form one basis for affirmative action in this respect, as Osler (1994) has pointed out. This can subsequently be used as the basis for action in the prescribed curriculum, to be considered later in this chapter.

Teaching is preoccupied with human interaction at a variety of levels. The working day brings teachers into regular, intense and long-term contact with children. This breeds familiarity, and an unquestioning approach in the classroom. Moreover, after initial training, very few opportunities exist for teachers to engage in critical reflection. This can lead to a belief that what has been successful in the past will continue to be so in the future, in spite of new social and educational conditions and the changing needs of the SEN population.

So, we have to determine what messages are being transmitted by our actions in the classroom. Are these messages inclined to encourage or discourage pupil participation? Are we conditioned into accepting an official, uniform vision of what constitutes a 'good' teacher, based upon the measurable 'outputs' of children rather than upon what they really need? A closer understanding of 'self' via the kind of reflection refined by Schon (1987) may lead to a growth in confidence to pursue classroom approaches which allow teachers to stand down from the hierarchical position that they have traditionally occupied. It may encourage unorthodox yet valid responses to learning situations which are generated by the children themselves. Risk-taking of this order requires time and space for all those involved to explore their own preconceptions and limits if it is not to end in failure.

In assessing where individual teachers stand in respect of classroom empowerment it is necessary to explore the tensions implicit in a teacher's role. Hammersley (1977) suggested that there were numerous contradictions in the work that teachers do. These included the process-product orientation of pupil learning, in which learning behaviour is assessed in terms of how an answer is reached rather than whether the answer is right. A second characteristic noted by Hammersley was the universalism-particularism dimension. This also suggests contrasting approaches: teachers are inclined to evaluate pupil behaviour or achievement either by agreed standards, as in National Curriculum testing, or by individual pupil performances and behaviour. Finally, Hammersley noted that a teacher's role was defined by a high level of control over pupil action as opposed to a more liberal, cooperative approach.

Whilst many teachers are able to strike an effective balance between these polar constructs, there is little doubt that the last 16 years has witnessed an official emphasis on product universalism. and a high level of pupil control, especially in SEN. This has been replicated in INSET activity. This is potentially damaging to the development of a classroom climate which encourages advocacy and self-advocacy.

Teaching is premised on power-dominance relationships (Harris, 1982). In participating as an active agent in these arrangements the teacher uses three areas of specialised knowledge to assume control. He or she has rudimentary (at least) knowledge of the nature of the teaching-learning process (for example, child psychology, social factors affecting the ways in which classrooms are managed, learning theory, and so on). Secondly, he or she has insights into the way in which the schooling process works, from basic organisational tasks (like how to fill in the register) to more complicated, philosophical matters (for example, the withdrawal of children who have learning difficulty from mainstream classes to work in small groups with a support teacher). Finally, the teacher will have specific subject-based knowledge, more so since the prescriptions of the National Curriculum. Each of these bodies of 'knowledge' can be used by teachers either to control or to empower children. Those who have SEN are especially vulnerable to their use as devices in ensuring the preservation of a status quo in which they have very little say. This has been particularly the case with children who are termed disruptive because they question what is being taught to them and the manner in which it is being presented.

Any alternative approach in INSET, which seeks to develop a greater understanding of the educational benefits of advocacy and self-advocacy and the skills necessary to promote them, needs to be justified on educational grounds. This can be done by concentrating on two aspects of a teacher's work: the curriculum and the way in which classrooms are organised and managed.

Curriculum, classrooms and the development of advocacy and self-advocacy

Access to the whole curriculum has been one of the cornerstones of curriculum planning in SEN for many years. Brennan (1979), for instance, referred to the need for balance and continuity in what was taught, themes amplified by the findings of the Warnock Committee (DES, 1978) and by DES (1984). More recently, NCC (1989) indicated that whilst the 1981 Education Act gave children who had SEN the right to share in the curriculum, this 'does not automatically ensure access to it, nor progress within it'. Access, progress and a 'share in the curriculum' are, in turn, synonymous with the concept of inclusivity, implying the empowerment of all participants, whether pupils or teachers. The rhetoric of official terminology disguises control rather than promotes self-advocacy. It needs to be swept aside. A teacher committed to advocacy and self-advocacy must provide the appropriate classroom climate for learning to take place and a range of strategies to enable the child who has SEN to participate in decision-making.

In Section One we noted that cooperation in the classroom actually promotes more efficient teaching and learning. Research in the United States into the effiectiveness of cooperative learning by Davidson (1990) and Slavin (1990) has shown that pupil performance is significantly enhanced when children learn in this way. In England, Foot *et al* .(1990) showed that cooperative tasks increased pupil performance in memory test scores, and Barron and Foot (1991) confirmed that 8-year-olds working in pairs performed better on spatial-numeric and item-recall tasks. Thus, in spite of a body of conflicting evidence (Light *et al.*, 1987), there is considerable support for classroom approaches which allow pupils to cooperate with each other.

Secondly, official directives have long stressed the need for teachers to take account of the individual learning characteristics of pupils. Differentiation, in this respect has assumed a central position in post-1988 educational jargon. But there has also developed a recognition that teachers have been less successful in identifying the personality characteristics they prefer to find in children. Taylor (1976), for example, showed that out of a range of 12 pupil-constructs produced by teachers, only two referred to the pupils' personality characteristics. As social encounters in classrooms are crucially significant in determining learning outcomes (Slavin, 1990), this has important implications. Undue emphasis upon academic differentiation, at the expense of personality differences, may therefore render formal curriculum intervention impotent.

Moreover, pupil management strategies have, according to Woods (1979), been based upon traditional means of control which are probably inadequate given the wide range of individual differences present in most contemporary classrooms. Such differences have increased markedly following the 1981 Education Act and teachers have had to devise alternative means of 'control'. Significant amongst these are negotiation and fraternisation. The former concerns the informal process by which a teacher and her pupils arrive at a consensus view on classroom order based upon her interpretation of formal school rules and procedures.

Fraternization, on the other hand has been described by Cohen and Manion (1981) as a teachers attempt to 'strive for good relations with one's pupils with a view to minimizing potential conflict and developing a sense of obligation in them' (p.121). Both approaches can help to create   a classroom climate which will provide opportunities for children to make decisions about their own learning.

Each of the above characteristics can be used for the benefit of the teacher and pupils, including, significantly, those who have SEN. Collaborative work, individualisation of learning programmes and effective classroom management are all attributes which have received official recognition in recent reports and guidelines concerning SEN. Each is an essential skill in the repertoire of an effective teacher, and all are accorded due status by OFSTED (1993). Accepting this official line, however, does not mean that teachers working with children who have SEN should simply use traditional strategies to secure acceptance.

Nowhere is this more apparent than in the way in which the National Curriculum is taught. *A Curriculum for All* (NCC, 1989) promoted an approach to subject-based teaching for children who had SEN which reaffirmed 'The principle that pupils with SEN share a common entitlement to a broad and balanced curriculum with their peers' (p.1). This rather extravagant claim for entitlement sits rather easily alongside the official view on assessment. In consequence many teachers, particularly in the mainstream, found that their best intentions were subverted by the demands placed upon them in a product-led curriculum.

But this is only half of the curriculum story. Thankfully there are sufficient examples of teachers (and whole schools) who have been able to empower the learner who has SEN. These can form a useful basis for individual teacher development. Ingram and Worrall (1993), for example, argue for a 'negotiating classroom', and suggest a number of straightforward ways in which this can be initiated. Brandes and Ginnis (1990), too, promote advocacy and self-advocacy within the formally taught curriculum, and again offer a wide-range of activities which teachers can draw upon. Nevertheless, it may be that the constraints of time and money and a need for teachers to be seen to be 'in control' may discourage some from attempting to work in this way.

Practical examples of the merits of listening to children are persuasive. A recent study (Garner, 1993b) showed how the views of 'disruptive pupils' could be used to promote effective teacher development. The views expressed by the pupils covered a range of curriculum topics, including subjects, teachers, teaching and learning styles and the organisation of the curriculum. It was striking that many of the views were expressed in a constructive way - a factor which could allay the fears of those reluctant to engage in such dialogues. The pupils' views, whether positive or negative, subsequently formed the basis of INSET sessions developed by the school.

An agreed framework for teacher development needs to be planned to ensure that a climate is fostered in which classrooms can become 'listening *and* hearing classrooms'. Whatever format such action takes, certain principles will help to ensure success. Those committed to pupil-empowerment should never give up. If a teacher opts out of discussion, persuasion and negotiation with colleagues, their views will simply be replaced by those of others who may have far less interest in challenging the status quo. In some schools, teachers who promote the involvement of SEN pupils in decision-making may initially be unpopular. They may be seen as 'trendy' and ill-advised to ignore the often repeated adage that if you give them an inch....

It is also essential to recognise that children who have SEN are empowered by being taught well. Whole-school strategies and good intentions will count for nothing if the necessary knowledge and skills to acquire status via learning are not transmitted effectively. Again, this is a stance which is validated by OFSTED (1993) and can be used to justify the alternative curriculum approaches.

Finally, in daily interactions with children teachers should try to avoid the traditional operations and messages which confirm the status and acceptability of competition to the exclusion of cooperative endeavour.

Using INSET to promote individual approaches to advocacy and self-advocacy.

The belief-systems which support the daily actions of teachers in SEN need to be reviewed and, at the very least, queried. Some teachers concerned with SEN children have stood rather idly by whilst successive governments have introduced policy initiatives which have done little more than confirm the behavioural model in both the social and the academic curriculum. Those involved in the education of pupils who have SEN have been unable to resist the catastrophic dismemberment of support services in the period after 1988. What is needed, therefore, is INSET which actually promotes the value of empowerment. This, it has to be said, will demand considerable courage on the part of the training providers and resilience, idealism and discernment on the part of those who participate.

What makes all of this regrettable is that, in recent literature concerning teacher education, there is very little evidence of any awareness that such programmes of individual development need to be undertaken. An informal review of current INSET provision in SEN conducted by one of the authors showed that there were few courses with a specific emphasis on the development of pupil empowerment. In a review of INSET (Tilstone, 1991), no mention is made of this interdependence, whilst HMI (1990), in an analysis of the content of Initial Teacher Training (ITT) courses, noted that little emphasis was given to advocacy matters. Consequently teachers may be very reluctant to promote empowerment among children if they have been given little opportunity to experience it themselves.

Dyson (1991) has argued that both the roles and concepts involved in working with children who have SEN should be rethought. Significant emphasis, he argued, should be placed upon a combination of critical reflection as refined by Schon (1987), and what he refers to as 'professional learning'. An acknowledgement is made that, in striking a balance between what have been viewed as contradictory stances (Fish *et al.* 1991),

> there are strong reasons why professionals such as special needs coordinators, who have a job to get on with and do, should concern themselves with the questions of effectiveness and efficiency which are most obviously relevant in the doing of that job (p. 51).

What is missing from this argument, however, is a recognition that many forms of INSET in SEN have moved towards a competence-*led* approach. The suggestion is that INSET has responded to the official needs of the professional community, rather than the intrinsic needs of the children themselves. This is particularly so in training connected with the SEN Code of Practice, behaviour management and curriculum intervention.

In order to advance matters, so that INSET activities can offer a platform for the development of advocacy and self-advocacy in schools, the concluding argument of this chapter is that teachers and training providers need to move away from an unquestioning allegiance to this recent style of INSET. Defining the dilemmas which surround work with children who have SEN will mean, at times, a painful exposure of what Harris (1982) has defined as 'fetished centres of unity', one of which is the belief that INSET should have an immediate 'pay off'. A growth of advocacy and self-advocacy in schools is incremental, and an isolated two-hour staff- development slot examining the views of children, which is submerged in the more usual pattern of reactive, procedural and utilitarian INSET, will do little to foster its growth. A more formal programme of awareness raising in advocacy and self-advocacy spread over a number of months, is needed in order to enable teachers to understand the value of the humanistic, empowering approach for those who have SEN.

As part of a modular INSET arrangement delivered by HE institutions, one possibility is for teacher educators and teachers to cooperate in the design of a module with the provisional title 'Teachers, Pupils and Empowerment'. The rationale for such a module, which could prove to be a persuasive factor in helping to secure financial support for its participants, is that collaborative schools are effective schools. The proposed module could function within a Diploma or Masters programme. It could include the following:

- Examination of personal beliefs and values
- Self-esteem in teaching and learning
- Interpersonal relationships in the classroom
- Sympathy and empathy
- Communication skills
- Self-advocacy in subject studies
- Children as decision-makers
- Rites of passage: children in society
- Parents, teachers and children together
- Coping with failure, coping with success
- Traditional organisations: classrooms and schools
- Listening to children
- Opportunities for inclusion
- Legal frameworks, rights and duties
- Conflict resolution.

But the content of such an INSET programme would only be effective if it provided opportunities for the kind of personal reflection referred to earlier. 'Baker days' in advocacy won't do. Teachers, at whatever level, need to view the kind of content suggested above from a critical distance. Supported and prompted by colleagues, they should be encouraged to explore ways of making their own classrooms happier and more productive places.

A further suggestion, based upon the need to establish a whole-school ethos is that, however expensive such a module might be, it would be at its most beneficial when everyone in a school participated. In doing this all members of staff would need to buy-in to the underpinning philosophy of the programme - that the views of children are valid, and that they should have the opportunity to express them.

Conclusion

As education has become increasingly ruled by market forces, we have suggested in this chapter that individual teachers have to make painful choices in respect of the INSET they undertake. On the one hand, they have to attend to the practical matters of their role, ensuring, for example, that the child who has SEN is provided with a wide range of curriculum opportunities. More problematically, perhaps, the conventions, belief-systems and attitudes which influence the way teachers work should be examined. This, we have argued, is a critical element in establishing a foundation for the growth of advocacy and self-advocacy. Teachers, working with children who have SEN, have therefore to exhume the humanistic, child-centredideology which has remained their bedrock and give it priority in their professional development.

CHAPTER 3.2

TOWARDS THE INCLUSIVE SCHOOL

The Code of Practice on the Identification and Assessment of Special Educational Needs (COP) (DfE, 1994) outlines a number of specific items for consideration when formulating a whole-school policy for SEN. In doing so the Code, which will probably be the last major official policy document this century regarding SEN, fails to acknowledge the debate concerning the very use of the term 'special educational needs'. Some professionals have begun to utilise the term 'inclusivity' (Norwich, 1993). They maintain that SEN is a term which suggests that the 'problem' remains with the child. The move towards inclusivity, on the other hand, places an emphasis upon the shortcomings of the educational system (Dyson, 1990). Quite apart from its moral efficacy, this focus is of particular concern at the present time, when competition for educational resources through local management of schools (LMS) means that the needs of pupils with SEN are less likely to be met.

Advocacy and self-advocacy are of immense importance to the development of an inclusive approach. An underlying, common theme in this book has been that the principles and practice of empowerment are applicable to all pupils, irrespective of their learning or social performances. This brings us close to the view held by Barton (1993) and others that the promotion of the term 'inclusive education' will be a potent weapon against those who 'give legitimation to individualistic, deficit views of the person'.

The previous chapter identified some of the issues which teachers could use as starting points or questions for reflection on their current approach to advocacy and self-advocacy. The success of such individual actions, however, will be proportionate to the institutional commitment to the inclusion of all children in decision making. As with other educational issues, this has come to be defined as a 'whole-school policy'. In the case of advocacy and self-advocacy for children who have SEN, however, the implications for the school extend far beyond its promotion solely within an SEN policy. The development of 'inclusivity' requires that the views of *all* children are given equal weight, and that all pupils in the school are given opportunities to make decisions on a wide range of educational matters. Chapter 2.3 exemplifies how this can be done.

The term 'whole-school policy' is one with which most teachers are now very familiar, whether in connection with equal opportunity, behaviour and discipline, reading, or the many other responsibilities currently facing teachers. In consequence, the importance of whole-school approaches in SEN has frequently been acknowledged (Daniels, 1984; Roaf, 1988; Wolfendale, 1987), and has been the subject of recent review in the light of SEN policy initiatives by central government (Palmer, *et al.*, 1994).

The current importance of whole-school approaches to SEN has been confirmed by OFSTED (1993). One of the primary considerations used by inspectors when reviewing evidence of satisfactory practice is that SEN provision should be 'based on an appropriate and effective whole school policy'. Part 4 of the Inspection Schedule notes that 'The policy should be drawn up by the governing body and senior management, helped by the expertise of suitable staff' and that 'All members of the teaching staff should be committed to its successful implementation' (p. 60).

The COP reinforces the statutory duty of all maintained schools to provide details of their policy for those children who have learning difficulties. An SEN policy, either in a preliminary, developmental stage or in its complete form must contain specific details regarding provision; for our purposes it should be noted that some of this requisite information relates directly to the promotion of advocacy and self-advocacy.

The COP is less than forthcoming on the question of pupil involvement however, this aspect of individual empowerment is largely overshadowed by copious descriptions of procedures (Garner, 1995). In the absence of more substantive official guidance to schools, the need to promote the views of pupils may be overlooked in the face of the countless other innovations required of teachers.

The difficulties facing those who have to implement changes to SEN policies in schools, so that they enable the pupils to participate more easily, are similar to those faced by any teacher who has responsibility for policy implementation in other aspects of school life (Pollard, 1994). One of these, undoubtedly, is innovation overload, or, as Bines (1993) prefers to call it, 'policy fatigue'. As more and more demands are placed on schools to respond to policy directives from central government, there can be a tendency to 'do' a policy, place it in written form on a shelf, and await the advent of OFSTED. Significantly, many teachers will, at one time or another, have complained about 'paper policies'. Policy statements are often exercises in rhetoric, having little impact on teaching and learning in the classroom.

At this point it should be noted that one of the key criteria used by OFSTED in assessing the quality of management in schools is that evaluations will be based on 'a comparison of the school's practice with the intentions expressed in its documentation' (OFSTED, 1993, Part 4, p. 64). It is therefore important that schools provide a framework for policy implementation by formulating a development plan based on practical ways of establishing inclusivity.

The school development plan has been widely recognised as an important device by which policy can be put into practice (Sammons and Stoll, 1990). The DfE describes a school development plan as 'a plan of needs for development set in the context of the school's aims and values, its existing achievements and national and LEA policies and initiatives'. The development plan comprises 'a map of the most suitable route to get to where the school or department wants to be' (Rogers, 1994). Based on this principle, development plans are now used in the evaluation of schools' management procedures (OFSTED, 1993).

Palmer, *et al.*, (1994) suggested that a school policy for SEN should consist of philosophy, principles, procedures and performance. We propose a development plan which adapts this and focuses on three areas:

- Philosophy: where are we all now and where would we all like to be?
- Practice: what are the aims, tasks and resources required to implement this philosophy?
- Performance: have we all got to where we wanted to go?

We have highlighted a range of considerations which schools need to address or review in order to promote advocacy and self-advocacy. A school development plan should begin by providing opportunities for all teachers, pupils, parents and others to examine what the school currently does to promote pupil involvement. Principles of inclusivity are about much more than just a whole school policy for SEN. Advocacy and self-advocacy can be promoted in many aspects of school life, not all of which are traditionally associated with SEN. They can include:

- school aims
- school council
- equal opportunities (including. anti-racist and anti-sexist)
- bullying
- parental involvement
- staffing flexibility
- curriculum flexibility and access
- uniform
- access to buildings
- assessment (including contribution to statements)
- discipline policy
- school charters
- standards of teaching
- school rules
- school organisation.

All those involved need to respond to two questions : 'What role do pupils play in the planning, practice and maintainence of our school's_____ policy?' and 'What new opportunities should be made available so that pupils can contribute to the school's_____ policy?' Each of these questions, phrased according to the intended audience, will enable the school to assess where it currently stands on matters of pupil empowerment and, perhaps more importantly, the extent to which it is prepared to take steps to secure wider participation. This leads to a third question, which relates directly to the collective philosophy of the school: 'Why do we need to change?'

Whilst it is relatively easy for a staff-meeting to be used to obtain the ostensible *views* of teachers about pupil participation, it is more difficult to convince them that advocacy and self-advocacy benefit everyone. It is also a more time-consuming exercise. In spite of these problems, it is none the less important for the headteacher and governors to accept that a development plan for inclusive education requires the involvement of everyone. Children and their parents are not being empowered if they do not have the opportunity to contribute to policy decisions! A development plan for advocacy and self-advocacy would present a poor role model for pupils if senior managers are perceived to be the sole agents of change.

Each area of school life listed above can be used as the focus for the promotion of advocacy and self-advocacy. For those who are sceptical of the merits of pupil inclusion in decision making, the most potent method of persuasion is an example of existing good practice. Many of these already exist either in individual classrooms, departments or schools, as suggested by the examples contained in Section Two of this book. If significant progress is to be continued, these successes must be given wide publicity. This can be done by recognising that dedicated INSET days are earmarked throughout the year; as we have suggested in Chapter 3.1, one-off sessions will not provide the necessary impetus for institutional change. On a larger scale, the practice of 'networking' between schools has become a lost art in the face of constraints imposed by LMS. It nevertheless remains a powerful device for institutional development (Bell and Dennis, 1994). Networking can ensure that news of successful programmes of pupil involvement reaches a wide audience, with the possibility that they can be used as starting points for institutional development. Both approaches are illustrated in the following example.

The Luke Bennett School is an 11-18 comprehensive school in the south-east of England, with over 900 pupils on roll. The school draws on a socially-mixed catchment area, and in 1993 had 21 pupils who had statements of SEN. Additionally there were 53 other children who were at earlier stages of assessment under the LEA's identification format for SEN. A decision was made by the senior management team (SMT), following general discussion in staff-meetings, to investigate the views of pupils about the school. A questionnaire was developed which focused upon four aspects of school life: the school environment and buildings; classroom organisation and management; the curriculum; non-timetabled time and the pastoral system. All pupils responded anonymously to the questionnaire. Some questionnaires were discreetly coded in order to ensure that the views of pupils who had learning difficulties could be ascertained.

As a result of this exercise, the school discovered that, compared with other children, pupils who had SEN felt that bullying was more of a problem and that some teachers were far less good at ensuring that the content of their lesson was made appropriate to the needs of the pupils. Moreover, one sub-group of SEN pupils, those who were perceived to have emotional or behavioural problems, noted that there were discrepancies in the application of school rules between the teachers. Several other important insights into the school experiences of this group of pupils were discovered. The information generated was used in a number of ways. Firstly, the results of the whole-school questionnaire were fed back to the pupils and parents, and were used as the basis for classroom discussions (for example, on rewards and punishments). The Pupil Council debated the outcomes of the questionnaire, and made suggestions to the SMT concerning changes to school organisation.

For the teachers, the results of the pupil survey meant that information became available about the way they taught and interacted with pupils. From a professional development point of view, such information was of critical importance. Prior to this exercise the teachers tended to make use of unofficial, anecdotal feedback from the pupils and, in some cases, embark on individual action plans to promote greater pupil participation. Now, however, substantial data were available concerning the views of pupils, including those with SEN, and this was used in staff development sessions in the succeeding months. Considerable emphasis was placed, for example, on the development of a wider range of learning styles, especially in science and mathematics, two subjects identified by the SEN pupils in the survey as not providing relevant or appropriate learning experiences. In all of this professional development, however, it was emphasised that changes in teaching and learning, in school organisation and in pastoral care, were being undertaken from a position of strength. The entire teaching staff of the school had the courage to examine its practices and, more importantly, to listen to the results of their investigation. The process is currently ongoing, but in becoming a 'listening school', Luke Bennett has taken an important step along the road to inclusivity. Moreover, two of the teaching staff from the school have presented INSET sessions to other local schools and several have expressed an interest in following this approach. This kind of networking will thus enable a local movement for advocacy and self-advocacy to be strengthened.

Of course each school, and the context in which it operates, will be different. Nevertheless, the example described above shows that even in the short term, and by using a very simple means of gathering information, significant steps can be made towards empowering pupils.

The development of a school which actively promotes the involvement of pupils in every aspect of their life in school is not a process which will occur either by osmosis or over a short period of time and by chance. The growth of advocacy and self-advocacy for pupils who have SEN will develop only by direct, unified action on the part of all those involved and by constant monitoring of the progress made. Schools are dynamic organisations, being subject to the effects of change from without and within. Axiomatically, the the strategies necessary to sustain continued pupil participation will need to be flexible. So it is essential that the question, 'Have we got to where we want to be?' is used frequently, and that it is directed to a wide audience.

From a national point of view there is little doubt that there has been a significant raising of awareness of the need to ensure advocacy and self-advocacy (Khaleel, 1993). Things have come a long way since pre-Warnock times, and there is now a widespread view that 'Any school which seeks to meet the needs of all its pupils will need to identify, address and constantly review the perceptions and evaluations of each of its pupils as individual human beings' (Tisdall and Dawson, 1994). But there is always a danger of complacency and that rhetoric will outstrip practice. Genuine pupil participation, in which the opinions offered by pupils with SEN are accepted as worthwhile and at face value, requires that teachers, parents and others continue to reflect on the status of advocacy and self-advocacy in schools. Those accepted landmarks for inclusive education - the 1981 Education Act, the UN Convention on the Rights of the Child, the Children Act, and the hint of advocacy and self-advocacy suggested by the COP - will continue to remain as pious philosophy unless those who interface most critically with children with learning difficulty - teachers in schools - feel motivated to adopt an inclusive approach to educational decision-making. That is the challenge which presents itself at the close of the century.

Ultimately the acid test for schools will be in the collective response of teachers, children, support staff, governors and parents to three questions. Have the children the right to express their own opinions about their social and academic life in school? Is there an organisational structure within the school which ensures that the opinions of children are listened to and taken seriously? And does action, based upon cooperative discussion between children and significant others, follow? A school which has adopted the principle of inclusivity will be able to respond positively to each question.

REFERENCES

Adams, R. (1991) *Protests by Pupils*, London: Falmer.

Ainscow, M. and Tweddle, D. (1979) *Preventing Classroom Failure: an objectives approach*, Chichester: Wiley.

Aries, P. (1962) *Centuries of Childhood* London: Jonathan Cape.

Armstrong D., Galloway, D. and Tomlinson, S. (1993) 'Assessing Special Educational Needs: the child's contribution', *British Educational Research Journal*, **19** (2), pp.121-131.

Arnot, M. and Barton, L.(eds) (1992) *Voicing Concerns*, Wallingford: Triangle Books.

Audit Commission, HM Inspectorate of Schools (1992) *Getting in on the Act: Provision for Pupils with Special Educational Needs: The national picture*, London: HMSO.

Barron, A-M. and Foot, H. (1991) 'Peer tutoring and tutor training',*Educational Research*, **33** (3), pp. 174-185.

Bartlett, N. (1989) 'The Children's Advocate', *Community Care*, 26.10.89, pp. 23-24.

Barton, L. (1991) 'Teachers under siege: A case of unmet needs', *Support for Learning*, **6** (1), pp. 3-8.

Barton, L. (1993) 'Labels, markets and inclusive education', in Visser, J. and Upton, G. (eds) *Special Education in Britain after Warnock*, London: David Fulton, pp. 30-42.

Barton, L. and Oliver, M. (1992) 'Special Needs: personal trouble or public issue', in Arnot, M. and Barton, L. (eds) *Voicing Concerns*, Wallingford: Triangle Books.

Bash, L. Coulby, D. and Jones, C. (1985) *Urban Schooling: Theory and Practice*, London: Cassell.

Bastiani, J. (1987) *Parents and Teachers 1. Perspectives on home-school relations*, Windsor: NFER-Nelson.

Bastiani, J. and Doyle, N. (1994) *Home and School: Building a better Partnership*, London : National Consumer Council.

Bell, G. and Dennis, S. (1994) 'School Development Networking and Managing for Change', in Bell, G., Stakes, R. and Taylor, G. (eds) *Action Research, Special Needs and School Development*, London: David Fulton.

Beresford, P. and Campbell, J. (1994) 'Disabled People, Service Users, User Involvement and Representation', *Disability and Society*, **9** (3), pp. 315-325.

Bewley, C. and Glendinning, C. (1994) 'Representing the Views of Disabled People in Community Care Planning', *Disability and Society*, **9** (3), pp. 301-314.

Bines, H. (1993) 'Whole School Policies in the New Era', *British Journal of Special Education*, **20** (3), pp. 91-94.

Boal, A. (1979) *Theatre of the Oppressed* , London: Pluto Press.

Bowers, T. (ed.) (1989) *Special Educational Needs and Human Resource Management*, Beckenham: Croom Helm.

Brandes, D. and Ginnis, P. (1990) *The Student-Centred School*, Oxford: Blackwell.

Brennan, W. (1979) *The Curricular needs of Slow Learners*, London: Evans Methuen Educational.

Britton, J. (1987) Vygotsky's Contribution to Pedagogical Theory. *English in Education*, **21**, (2).

Campbell, A. (ed.) (1938) *Modern Trends in Education*, Report of the Proceedings of the New Education Fellowship Conference, Wellington: Whitcombe and Tombs.

Clifford, B. (1993) 'Witnessing: a comparison of adults and children'. *Issues in Criminological and Legal Psychology*, **20**, pp. 15-21.

Cohen, L. and Manion, L. (1981) *Perspectives on Classrooms and Schools*, London : Cassell Education.

Cooper, C. (1992) 'Putting People First', *Community Care*, 13.8.92, pp. 20-21.

Cooper, P. (1993) 'Learning from Pupils' Perspectives', *British Journal of Special Education*, **20** (4), pp. 29-133.

Cornish, D. and Clarke, R. (1975) *Residential Treatment and its Effects on Delinquency*, London : HMSO.

Council for the Accreditation of Teacher Education (1992) *Initial Teacher Training (Secondary Phase)*, Circular 9/92. London: DfE.

Coulby, J. (1986) 'A Practical Approach to Behaviour in the Primary School', *Primary Teaching Studies*, **1** (3), pp. 91-97.

Coulby, J. and Coulby, D. (1990) 'Interviewing in Junior Classroom', in Docking, J. (ed.) *Education and Alienation in the Junior School*, London : Falmer.

Cox, C. and Dyson, A. (eds) (1969) *Fight for Education: A Black Paper*, London : Critical Quarterly Society.

Cronk, K. (1987) *Teacher-Pupil Conflict in Secondary Schools*, London: Falmer.

Curtis, M. (1983)Social Skills Training in the Classroom, *Behavioural Approaches With Children*, **7**, pp. 3-17.

Dalrymple, J. (1993) 'Advice, advocacy and representation for children', *Childright*, **98**, pp. 1-13.

Daniels, E. (1984) 'A suggested model for remedial provision in a comprehensive school', *Remedial Education*, **19** (2), pp. 78-83.

Darling, J. (1994) *Child-Centred Education*, London: Paul Chapman.

Davidson, N. (1990) Cooperative learning research in mathematics. Paper delivered to *IACSE 5th International Convention on Cooperative Learning*, Baltimore, MD, July.

Davie, R. (1993) 'Children with emotional and behavioural difficulties', Paper given to *National Children's Bureau Conference*, March.

Davies, G. (1983) 'An Introduction to Life and Social Skills Training', *Journal of Maladjustment and Therapeutic Education*, **1**, pp. 13-21.

Davis, C. and Stubbs, R. (1989) *Shared Reading in Practice*, Buckingham: Open University Press.

Davis, M. and Long, T. (1983) *Role Play for English and PSE*, Oxford : Basil Blackwell.

Dearing, R. (1993a) *The National Curriculum and its Assessment: Interim Report*, York/London : NCC/SEAC.

Dearing, R. (1993b) *The National Curriculum and its Assessment: Final Report*, London: SCAA.

Department for Education (1993) *Interim Report on the National Curriculum and its Assessment: The Government's Response*, London: DFE.

Department for Education (1994a) *Code of Practice on the identification and assessment of special educational needs*, London: DfE.

Department for Education (1994b) *Special Educational Needs Agenda for Parents*, London: DfE.

Department for Education (1994c) *Special Needs Tribunals: how to appeal*, London: DfE.

Department for Education (1994d) *Pupil Behaviour and Discipline*, Circular 8/94, London: DfE.

Department for Education (1994e) *The Parent's Charter*. London: DfE.

Department of Education and Science (1967) *Children and their Primary School* s ('The Plowden Report'), London: HMSO.

Department of Education and Science (1978) *Special Educational Needs - Report of the Committee of Enquiry into the Education of Handicapped Children and Young People* ('The Warnock Report'), London: HMSO.

Department of Education and Science (1984) *The Initial Training of Teachers: approval of courses.* Circular 3/84. London: DES.

Department of Education and Science (1985) *Better Schools*, London : HMSO.

Department of Education and Science (1989) *Discipline in Schools* ('The Elton Report'), London: HMSO.

Department of Education and Science (1991), updated by DFE 1994d) *The Parent's Charter*, London: DES.

Department of Education and Science (1990) *Special Educational Needs in Initial Teacher Training.* London: DES.

Department of Education and Science (1992) *Choice and Diversity - a new framework for schools*, London: HMSO.

Dewey, J. (1916) *Democracy and Education*, New York: Macmillan.

Dyson, A. (1985) 'A Curriculum for the 'Educated Man'?', *British Journal of Special Education*, **12** (4) , pp.138-139.

Dyson, A. (1990) 'Special educational needs and the concept of change', *Oxford Review of Education*, **16** (1), pp. 55-66.

Dyson, A. (1991) 'Rethinking roles, rethinking concepts: Special needs teachers in mainstream schools', *Support for Learning*, **6** (2), pp. 51-60.

Edwards, D. and Mercer, N. (1987) *Common Knowledge: The Development of Understanding in the Classroom*, London: Routledge.

Feldman, D (1993) *Civil Liberties and Human Rights in England and Wales*, Oxford : Clarendon Press.

Fish, D., Twinn, S. and Purr, B. (1991) *Promoting Reflection : Improving the supervision of practice in health visiting and initial teacher training*, Twickenham: West London Institute of Higher Education.

Fleming, M. (1994) *Starting Drama Teaching*, London: David Fulton.

Foot, H., Morgan, M. and Shute, R. (eds) (1990) *Children Helping Children*, Chichester: Wiley.

Franklin, B. (1986) 'Children's political rights', in B. Franklin (ed.) *The Rghts of Children*, Oxford; Blackwell.

Froebel, F. (1926) *The Education of Man*, New York: Appleton.

Furtwengler, W. (1985) 'Implementing Strategies for a School Effectiveness Program', *Phi Delta Kappan*, December, pp. 262-265.

Gains, C. (1994) 'Editorial', *Support for Learning*, **9** (4), p.102.

Galletley, I. (1985) 'Vocationalism must come first', *British Journal of Special Education*, **12** (4) , pp. 140-141.

Galloway, D., Ball, T., Blomfield, D. and Seyd, R. (1982) *Schools and Disruptive Pupils*, London: Longman.

Garner, P. (1992) 'Involving 'disruptive' students in school discipline structures', *Pastoral Care in Education*, **10** (3), pp. 13-19.

Garner, P. (1993a) A Comparative Study of Disruptive Students in England and the United States, unpublished PhD thesis, University of London.

Garner, P. (1993b) 'What disruptive students say about the school curriculum and the way it is taught', *Therapeutic Education and Care*, **2** (2), pp. 404-415.

Garner, P. (1993c) 'Special Education in Slovakia : a case-study of childrens' views', *International Journal of Special Education*, **8** (2), pp. 123-133.

Garner, P. (1995) 'Sense or Nonsense? *British Journal of Learning Support*, **10** (1), pp. 3-7.

Gersch, I. (1992) 'Pupil involvement in assessment' in Cline, T. (ed.)*The Assessment of Special Educational Needs: International Perspectives*, London: Routledge.

Gersch, I. and Cutting, M. (1985) 'The Child's Report', *Educational Psychology in Practice*, **1** (2), pp . 63-69.

Gersch, I. and Nolan, A. (1994): 'Exclusions - What the pupils think', *Educational Psychology in Practice*, **10** (1), pp. 35 - 45.

Gersch, I. Holgate, A. and Sigston, A. (1993) 'Valuing the Child's Perspective: A revised student report and other practical initiatives', *Educational Psychology in Practice*, **9** (1), pp. 36-45.

Gersch, I., Lockhart, R, Gersch, A. and Hooper, S. *The Child Witness Pack : an evaluation*, (In preparation).

Gersch, I. (1987) 'Involving Pupils in their own Assessment', in Bowers, T. (ed.) *Special Educational Needs and Human Resource Management*, Beckenham: Croom Helm. pp. 49-170.

Gersch, I. and Holgate, A. (1994) *The Student Report*, London Borough of Waltham Forest.

Gersch, I. (1990) 'The Pupil's view', in Scherer M., Gersch, I. and Fry, L.(ed.) *Meeting Disruptive Behaviour: Assessment, Intervention and Partnership,* London: Macmillan Education Ltd.

Gersch, I. and Noble, J. (1991) 'A Systems project involving students and staff in a secondary school', *Educational Psychology in Practice,* **7** (3), pp. 40-147.

Gipps, C. and Murphy, P. (1994) *A Fair Test? Assessment, achievement and Equity,* Buckingham: Open University Press.

Haigh, G. (1994) 'Voices of Reason', *TES Section 2,* 27. 5. 94, pp. 1-2.

Hammersley, M. (1977) *Teacher Perspectives, Open University Educational Studies, A Second Level Course (E202),* Milton Keynes: Open University.

Harris, R. (1982) *Teachers and Classes: A Marxist Analysis,* London : Routledge.

Hegarty, S. (1993) 'Home-school relations: a perspective from special education.', in Munn, P. (ed.) *Parents and Schools: Customers, Managers or Partners?,* London: Routledge.

Hellier, C. (1994) 'Closing the gap: Compensating for literacy delay in children with specific learning difficulties/dyslexia', *Support for Learning* , 9 (4), pp .162-165.

Hohman, M., Barnet, B. and Weikart, D. (1979) *Young Children in Action,* Ipsilanti, Michigan: High Scope Press.

Hughes, S. (1984) *An Evening at Alfie's.* London: The Bodley Head.

Hudson, B. (1989) 'Michael Lipsky and Street Level Bureacracy : a neglected perspective', in Barton, L. (ed.) *Disability and Dependency.* London : Falmer Press.

Illich, I. (1973) *Deschooling Society,* Harmondsworth: Penguin.

Ingram, J. and Worrall, N. (1993) *The Negotiating Classroom: Teacher and Child Partnership,* London: Fulton.

Jeffs, T. (1986) 'Children's rights at school', in Franklin, B. (ed.) *The Rghts of Children,* Oxford: Blackwell.

Johnson, L. and O'Neill, C. (1984) *Dorothy Heathcote: Collected Writings on Education and Drama,* London; Hutchinson.

Khaleel, M. (1993) *Pupil Councils: First Independent Monitoring Programme,* Liverpool: Priority Area Development.

Kingston Friends (1989) *Ways and Means,* Kingston: Kingston Friends Workshop.

Knight, P. (1992) 'Secondary schools in their own words: the image on school prospectuses', *Cambridge Journal of Education,* **22**, pp. 55-67.

Lawlor, S. (1990) *Teachers Mistaught: training theories or education in subjects*, London: Centre for Policiy Studies.

Light, P., Foot, T., Colburn, C. and McClelland, I. (1987) 'Collaborative interactions at the microcomputer keyboard', *Educational Psychology*, **7**, pp. 13-21.

Lindsay, M. (1992) 'An introduction to Children's Rights', *Highlight*, 113, London: National Children's Bureau.

Lipsky, M. (1980) *Street Level Bureacracy: Dilemmas of the Individual in Public Services*, Russell Sage Foundation: New York.

Lister, I. (ed..) (1972) *Deschooling*, Cambridge: Cambridge University Press.

Lister, I. (1991) 'The Challenge of Human Rights for Education', in Starkey, H. (ed.) *The Challenge of Human Rights Education* , London : Council of Europe/Cassell.

MaClure, M., Phillips,T. and Wilkinson, A. (eds.) (1988)*Oracy Matters*, Buckingham: Open University Press.

Mercer, N. (1990) 'Neo-Vygotskian Theory and Classroom Education', in Pike, G. and Selby, D. (eds) *Global Teacher; Global Learner*, London: Hodder & Stoughton, pp. 97-110.

Morgan, N. and Saxton, J. (1987) *Teaching Drama*, London, Hutchinson.

Murray, N. (1993) 'Wit and Wisdom'. *Community Care*, 18.11.93., p. 24.

NCC (1989) *Curriculum Guidance Two. A Curriculum for All, York*: NCC.

National Exclusions Reporting System (1992) (NERS) London: DfE.

National Union of Teachers (1993) *Survey of Local Authority Support Services*, London: NUT.

NCC (1990) *The Arts 5-16 A Curriculum Framework*, London : Oliver and Boyd.

Neelands, J. (1992) *Learning through Imagined Experience*, London: Hodder and Stoughton.

Nolan, A. and Sigston , A. (1993) *Where do I go from here? A booklet for students who have been excluded from school*, The London Borough of Waltham Forest.

Norwich, B. (1993) 'Has "Special Educational Needs" outlived its Usefulness?', in Visser, J. and Upton, G. (eds) *Special Education in Britain after Warnock*, London: David Fulton, pp. 43-58.

O'Neill, C., Lambert, A., Linnell, R. and Warr-Wood, J. (1976) *Drama Guidelines*, London: Heinemann.

Office for Standards in Education (1993a) *The Management and Provision of Inservice Training Funded by the Grant for Education and Support,* London: OFSTED.

Office for Standards in Education (1993b) *School Inspection Manual,* London: HMSO.

Oliver, M. (1990) *The Politics of Disablement,* Basingstoke, Macmillan.

Osler, A. (1994) 'The UN Convention on the Rights of the Child: some implications for teacher education', *Educational Review,* 46 (2), pp. 141-150.

Palmer, C., Redfern, R. and Smith, K. (1994) 'The Four P's of Policy', *British Journal of Special Education,* 21 (1), pp. 4-6.

Parsons, B., Schaffner, M., Little, G. and Felton, H. (1984) *Drama, Language and Learning,* Tasmania: NADIE.

Pestalozzi, J. (1826) '*Pestalozzi's theoretical and practical method for elementary education and instruction*', Samtliche Werke, 28, Zurich, Orell Fussli Verlag.

Peter, M. (1991) 'Progress Reports on Curriculum Change', *British Journal of Special Education,* 18 (4), p. 162.

Peter, M. (1994) *Drama for All: Developing drama in the curriculum with pupils with special educational needs,* London : David Fulton.

Peters, R. (1969) *Perspectives on Plowden,* London: Routledge and Kegan Paul.

Pike, G. and Selby, D. (eds) (1990) *Global Teacher; Global Learner,* London: Hodder & Stoughton.

Plotnikoff, J. (1993) *The Child Witness Pack,* London: NSPCC/ChildLine.

Pollard, A. (1994) 'Back to some different "basics" : Issues for the National Curriculum at Key Stage 2', in Pollard, A. (ed.) *Look Before You Leap? Research Evidence for the Curriculum at Key Stage Two,* London: Tufnell Press.

Reynolds, D. (1985) *Studying School Effectiveness,* Lewes : Falmer.

Reynolds, D. (1989) 'School Effectiveness and School Improvement : A Review of the British Literature', in Reynolds, D., Creemers, B. and Peters, T. (eds) *School Effectiveness and Improvement,* Cardiff: Cardiff University College, School of Education.

Riddell, S., Brown, S. and Duffield, J. (1994) 'Parental power and Special Educational Needs: the case of specific learning difficulties', *British Educational Research Journal,* 20 (3), pp. 327-344.

Roaf, C. (1988) 'The Concept of a Whole School Approach to Special Needs', in Robinson, O. (ed.) *Tackling Learning Difficulties.*, London : Hodder & Stoughton.

Rogers, C. (1969) *Client Centered Therapy: current practice implications and theory*, London: Constable.

Rogers, R. (1980) *Crowther to Warnock: how fourteen reports tried to change children's lives*, London: Heinemann.

Rogers, R. (ed.) (1994) *How to Write a School Development Plan*, London: Heinemann.

Rosenbaum, M. and Newell, P. (1991) *Taking Children Seriously: A proposal for a Children's Rights Commissioner*, London: Calouste Gulbenkian Foundtion.

Rowe, J. (1993) 'Educating Children In Care: a practitioner's perspective, unpublished MEd Thesis, Brunel University.

Sammons, P. and Stoll, L. (1990) 'Some Implications for Education Management of Findings from the ILEA's Junior School Project', in Saran, R. and Trafford, V. (eds) *Research in Education Management and Policy: Retrospect and Prospect*, London: Falmer.

Sandow, S. (1995) 'The Good King Dagobert, or Clever, Stupid, Nice, Nasty', Paper given at the *International Special Education Conference*, Birmingham, April.

Sandow, S. and Garner, P. (1994) 'No more saints, fools and gaolors : defining a new role for special educators', in Lawrence, I. (ed.) *Education Tomorrow*, London: Cassell.

Sandow, S., Stafford, D. and Stafford, P. (1986) *An Agreed Understanding?* Windsor: NFER-Nelson.

Schon, D. (1987) *Educating the Reflective Practitioner: Toward a new design for teaching and learning in the professions*, Oxford : Jossey Bass.

Schostak, J. (1983) *Maladjusted Schooling*, London: Falmer.

Searle, C. (1994) *Outcast England*, Paper given at the Centre for Education Welfare Studies, University of Huddersfield, June.

Seely, J. (1978) *In Role*, London: Edward Arnold.

Sheppard, B. (1988) *Off-site pupils and their experiences of schooling*, London: London University, Institute of Education Post-16 Education Centre.

Slavin, R. (1990) *Cooperative Learning: Theory, Research and Practice*, Englewood Cliffs, NJ: Prentice Hall.

Smith, C and Laslett, R. (1993) *Effective Classroom Management*, London: Routledge.

Spence, S. (1980) *Social Skills Training with Children and Adolescents: A Counsellor's Manual*, Windsor : NFER-Nelson.

Steirer, B. and Maybin, J. (eds) (1994) *Language, Literacy and Learning in Educational Practice*, Buckingham: Open University Press.

Stevenson, D. (1991) 'Deviant Students as a Collective Resource in Classroom Control', *Sociology of Education*, **64**, pp.127-133.

Stobart, G. (1986) 'Is integrating the handicapped psychologically defensible?', *Bulletin of the British Psychological Society*, **39**, pp. 1-3.

Sweeney, T. and Catt, R. (1993) 'Training the Detectives', *Language and Learning*, March, pp.14-18.

Taylor, M. (1976) 'Teachers' perceptions of their pupils', *Research in Education*, **16**, November, pp. 25-35.

Thomas, D. (1993) 'Gritty, sensible and utilitarian - the only model? Special educational needs, initial teacher training and professional development', in Dyson, A. and Gains, C. (eds) *Rethinking Special Needs in Mainstream Schools*, London: David Fulton.

Tilstone, C. (1991) 'Teacher education: The changing focus', in Ashdown, R., Carpenter, B. and Bovair, K. (eds) *The Curriculum Challenge*, London: Falmer.

Tisdall, G. and Dawson, R. (1994) 'Listening to the children : Interviews with children attending a mainstream support facility', *Support for Learning*, **9** (4), pp. 179-182.

Tomlinson, S. (1981) *Educational Subnormality - A Study in Decision Making*, London: Routledge and Kegan Paul.

Tomlinson, S. (1982) *A Sociology of Special Education*, London: Routledge and Kegan Paul.

Topping, K. (1992) 'Cooperative learning and peer tutoring: An overview', *The Psychologist*, April.

Tutt, N. (1978) *Alternative Strategies for Coping with Crime*, Oxford: Blackwell.

Tyne, A. (1994) 'Taking responsibility and giving power', *Disability and Society*, **9** (2), pp. 249-254.

Wagner, B. J. (1976) *Dorothy Heathcote: Drama as a Learning Medium*, Washington, DC: National Education Association.

Walford, G. (1994) 'The Dilemma of Choice in Education', in Lawrence, I. (ed.) *Education Tomorrow*, London: Cassell.

Wallwork, A. (1990) 'Chance or Choice', *British Journal of Special Education*, **17** (4), pp. 148-150.

Warnock, M. (1991) 'Equality fifteen years on', *Oxford Review of Education*, **17**,(2), pp. 145-153.

Weatherley, R. and Lipsky, M. (1977) 'Street level bureaucrats and institutional innovation ; implementing special education reform', *Harvard Educational Review*, **47**, pp. 171-197.

Weber, K. (1982) *The Teacher is the Key*, Buckingham: Open University Press.

Westmacott, E. and Cameron, R. (1984) *Behaviour Can Change*, Basingstoke: Globe Education.

Whitney, B. (1993) *The Children Act and Schools*, London: Kogan Page.

Wiltshire Oracy Project (1989) *Oracy in Action: a video-based training package on Oracy in Secondary Schools, Talking as Expert*, Swindon: Wiltshire Oracy Project.

Wolfendale, S. (1987) *Primary Schools and Special Needs: Policy, Planning and Provision*, London: Cassell.

Wolfensberger, W. and Menolascino, F. (1970) 'A Theoretical Framework for the Management of Parents of the Mentally Retarded', in Menolascino, F. (ed.) *Psychiatric Approaches to Mental Retardation*. New York: Basic Books.

Wolfensberger, W. (1989) 'Human Service Policies: the rhetoric versus the reality', in Barton, L. (ed.) *Disability and Dependency*. London: Falmer.

Wolfensberger, W. (1994) 'The Growing Threat to the Lives of Handicapped People in the Context of Modernistic Values', *Disability and Society* , **9** (3), pp. 395-413.

Wood, D. (1990) *How Children Think and Learn* Oxford : Blackwell.

Woods, P. (1979)*The Divided School*, London: Routledge and Kegan Paul.

Wragg, E.C. (ed.) (1984) *Classroom Teaching Skills: the research findings of the Teacher Education Project*, Beckenham; Croom Helm.

AUTHOR INDEX